Closing the Security Gap
Building Irregular Security Forces

by

Michael J. Gunther, Major, US Army

M.A., American Military University, Charles Town, West Virginia, 2005

B.S., United States Military Academy, West Point, New York, 2002

Fort Leavenworth, Kansas

Abstract

The British and US experience with the use of local, irregular security forces suggest their importance in assisting the host nation government and counterinsurgent forces. Their successful establishment, training, and employment demonstrate the importance of several prerequisites including partnership with an advisory force, consent of the host nation's government to exist, and that the security force is accountable to the local civil authority. Without these prerequisites, the local, irregular security force could risk illegitimacy in the eyes of the populace, the host nation government, and the counterinsurgent. However, partnership does not guarantee a local irregular force's success. The host nation's involvement in the decision to build irregular forces is important from the beginning of the campaign. Through the examination of archival research and primary source interviews associated with the British experience in North-West Frontier and the Dhofar region of Oman, one can start to understand the prerequisites needed to create a successful mentorship force. The paper examines the method of partnership, selection and traits of the advisors, and the host nation government's role in building the Punjab Irregular Force and Frontier Corps in the North-West Frontier in India, the firqat in Dhofar, and the Sons of Iraq.

Objectives of the Art of War Scholars Program

The Art of War Scholars Program is a laboratory for critical thinking. It offers a select group of students a range of accelerated, academically rigorous graduate level courses that promote analysis, stimulate the desire for life-long learning, and reinforce academic research skills. Art of War graduates will not be satisfied with facile arguments; they understand the complexities inherent in almost any endeavor and develop the tools and fortitude to confront such complexities, analyze challenges, and independently seek nuanced solutions in the face of those who would opt for cruder alternatives. Through the pursuit of these outcomes, the Art of War Scholars Program seeks to improve and deepen professional military education.

The Art of War Program places contemporary operations (such as those in Iraq and Afghanistan) in a historical framework by examining earlier military campaigns. Case studies and readings have been selected to show the consistent level of complexity posed by military campaigns throughout the modern era. Coursework emphasizes the importance of understanding previous engagements in order to formulate policy and doctrinal response to current and future campaigns.

One unintended consequence of military history education is the phenomenon of commanders and policy makers "cherry picking" history—that is, pointing to isolated examples from past campaigns to bolster a particular position in a debate, without a comprehensive understanding of the context in which such incidents occurred. This trend of oversimplification leaves many historians wary of introducing these topics into broader, more general discussion. The Art of War program seeks to avoid this pitfall by a thorough examination of context. As one former student stated: "The insights gained have left me with more questions than answers but have increased my ability to understand greater complexities of war rather than the rhetorical narrative that accompanies cursory study of any topic."

Professor Michael Howard, writing "The Use and Abuse of Military History" in 1961, proposed a framework for educating military officers in the art of war that remains unmatched in its clarity, simplicity, and totality. The Art of War program endeavors to model his plan:

Three general rules of study must therefore be borne in mind by the officer who studies military history as a guide to his profession and who wishes to avoid pitfalls. First, he must study in width. He must observe the way in which warfare has developed over a long historical period. Only by seeing what does change can one deduce what does not; and as much as can be learnt from the great discontinuities of military history as from the apparent similarities of the techniques employed by the great captains through the ages....Next he must study in depth. He should take a single campaign and explore it thoroughly, not simply from official histories, but from memoirs, letters, diaries. . . until the tidy outlines dissolve and he catches a glimpse of the confusion and horror of real experience... and, lastly, he must study in context. Campaigns and battles are not like games of chess or football matches, conducted in total detachment from their environment according to strictly defined rules. Wars are not tactical exercises writ large. They are...conflicts of societies, and they can be fully understood only if one understands the nature of the society fighting them. The roots of victory and defeat often have to be sought far from the battlefield, in political, social, and economic factors which explain why armies are constituted as they are, and why their leaders conduct them in the way they do.... It must not be forgotten that the true use of history, military or civil... is not to make men clever for the next time; it is to make them wise forever.

Gordon B. Davis, Jr.
Brigadier General, US Army
Deputy Commanding General
    CAC LD&E

Daniel Marston
DPhil (Oxon) FRHistS
Ike Skelton Distinguished Chair
  in the Art of War
US Army Command & General
  Staff College

Acknowledgments

I would like to acknowledge the assistance, guidance, and support of many people that made this thesis possible. First and foremost, I am deeply indebted to my wife, Heather, who has supported my academic pursuits no matter how many dinners, weekends, and events that are ruined by the arrival of new books. Thanks are due to my teammates, Darrell, Eric, Marcus, and Stew, who provided assistance and friendship in the face of adversity. I am deeply indebted to the many British veterans of the Dhofar campaign that shared their stories with our particular group of Americans. A special thanks to Dr. Marston, Dr. Murray, and Dr. Stephenson and the countless other supporters of the Art of the War Scholars program that have provided mentorship, advice, and support during the year. Additionally, I would like to thank several people that made our research ion the UK possible, including the archivists at the Middle East Centre, St. Antony's College, Oxford, the Liddell Hart Centre for Military Archives, King's College, London, and the British Library.

This thesis is the culmination of a conversation that started in Baghdad during the surge. Special thanks to Lt. Col. John Meyer, III and Maj. John Nakata for starting the dialogue and giving me something to think about for the last four years.

Finally, this thesis is dedicated to the memory of the five Soldiers of Mortar Platoon, 1-26 Infantry, 1st Infantry Division that died on 8 July 2004 in Samarra, Iraq while partnering with the 202nd Iraqi National Guard Battalion.

Table of Contents

Illustrations

Acronyms

ALP	Afghan Local Police
AQI	Al-Qaeda in Iraq
BATT	British Army Training Team
BL	British Library
CAP	Combined Action Platoon
CLC	Concerned Local Citizen
CO	Commanding Officer
COIN	Counterinsurgency
Col.	Colonel
CSAF	Commander, Sultan's Armed Forces
DLA	Dhofar Liberation Army
DLF	Dhofar Liberation Front
EIC	East India Company
FATA	Federally Administered Tribal Areas
FID	Foreign Internal Defense
FLOSY	Front for the Liberation of Occupied South Yemen
FM	Field Manual
FMI	Field Manual Interim
GPMG	General-Purpose Machine Gun
HMSO	His/Her Majesty's Stationary Office
IOR	India Office Records
ISAF	International Security Assistance Force
LHCMA	Liddell Hart Centre for Military Archives
Lt.	Lieutenant
Lt. Col.	Lieutenant Colonel
M2T	Monitor, Mentor, Train
Maj.	Major
MEC	Middle East Centre
MIKE	Mobile Strike Force Command
MiTT	Military Transition Team
MNF-I	Multi-National Forces-Iraq
NATO	North Atlantic Treaty Organization
NCO	Non-commissioned Officer

NLF	National Liberation Front
NWF	North-West Frontier
NWFP	North-West Frontier Province
OIOC	Oriental and India Office Collections
PDRY	People's Democratic Republic of Yemen
PFF	Punjab Frontier Force
PFLOAG	Popular Front, Liberation of the Occupied Arabian Gulf
PIF	Punjab Irregular Force
PSYOP	Psychological Operations
SAF	Sultan's Armed Forces
SAS	Special Air Service
SEP	Surrendered Enemy Personnel
SOAF	Sultan of Oman's Air Force
SoI	Sons of Iraq
TOS	Trucial Oman Scouts
UK	United Kingdom
US	United States
VCO	Viceroy's Commissioned Officer

Chapter 1

Introduction

The necessity of having a small force, acquainted with localities,
at the command of the Civil Authority in a new country, bordering
on troubled districts, is too apparent to require comment.

- Colonel Sir Henry Lawrence
to the Government of India, 7 June 1846.

Colonel Lawrence's[1] note to the Viceroy of India made the point that
in 1846 the use of local irregular forces[2] to assist the government was
self-apparent.[3] The British and US experience of building and partnering
with local, irregular security forces suggest their importance in assisting
the host nation government and counterinsurgent forces. Their successful
establishment, training, and employment demonstrate the importance of
several prerequisites including partnership with an advisory force, consent
of the host nation's government to exist, and that the security force is
accountable to the local civil authority. Without these prerequisites, the
local, irregular security force could risk illegitimacy in the eyes of the
populace, the host nation government, and the counterinsurgent.

Over 150 years later, the current operations in Iraq and Afghanistan
have highlighted partnership operations with indigenous forces. However,
the civil and military commands responsible for directing both campaigns
failed to develop a policy for partnership with regular and irregular forces
early in the wars. The US and the UK eventually developed transition
teams to partner with host nation regular security forces in 2005 and
2008 respectively.[4] The 2007 edition of US Field Manual (FM) 3-24:
Counterinsurgency devoted a chapter to the development of host nation
security forces for the first time.[5] Authors of subsequent manuals, articles,
and lectures listed best tactical practices, training challenges, and advisor
traits, but failed to highlight the strategic and operational importance of
partnership missions with local irregular forces. Thus, Colonel Lawrence's
lesson seemed lost in time. As a result, the US and UK failed to resource
the advisory missions for success. This failure is surprising given the fact
that the recruiting, training, and employing of indigenous forces were not
entirely new concepts in 2003 despite their absence from the doctrine.
During the last two hundred years the British and Americans have used
indigenous irregular forces, with varying degrees of success, to control
populations, provide internal security, and counterinsurgencies spanning
the Punjab, South Africa, Philippines, Malaya, Dhofar, Vietnam, and Iraq.[6]

Counterinsurgents create local irregular security forces as a common method of population control.[7] Often familiar or tribal ties, business, or proximity can tie a locally raised force to the populace. Irregular forces can assist the counterinsurgent with local population control by providing security for the population, intelligence collection, and law enforcement. Additionally, the local security force can assist the regular forces by providing information about the local people, culture, and terrain. In 1846, Colonel Lawrence proposed the formation of an irregular guide force because the British troops operating in the Punjab during the First Sikh War lacked information on roads, tribal allegiances, and the ability to communicate with the local populace. He did not want to repeat the situation in a future conflict. He realized that an irregular force could assist the local power, or counterinsurgent, with cultural norms, identify insurgents and abnormal activity, and assess the needs of the populace.[8]

Partnership[9] can increase training, discipline, leadership, and security force legitimacy by tying it to the government or interventionist power. However, partnership, in and of itself, does not guarantee a local irregular force's success. The partnership model needs to include the selection of personnel that are uniquely suited for the unique task of working with irregular security forces. Without selection criteria, the security force could fail to gain legitimacy, making it a liability to the counterinsurgent and the host nation. Colonel Lawrence understood the importance of advisor selection in June 1846. He wrote the Governor-General requesting oversight of officer selection for the new irregular force because, "As much of the success of the scheme proposed in this letter will depend on the officers selected."[10]

Consent of the host nation for the formation and employment of local irregular force is a second, equally important criterion to the partnership model in determining an irregular force's success. The Westphalian system of states has three primary tenets, the sovereignty of states and their fundamental right to political self-determination, the legal equality between states without regard to size, population, or influence, and the principle of non-intervention of one state in the internal affairs of another state.[11] A counterinsurgent that builds an irregular force without permission of the host government violates these principles. The counterinsurgent must convince the host government that the force is necessary, or the force's legitimacy is susceptible.[12] However, irregular forces created with the cooperation of the host nation's government can eventually be incorporated into the nation's security apparatus as regular forces. This scenario occurred with the Punjab Irregular Force in the North-West

Frontier from 1846 to 1945, and to a lesser extent with the *firqat* during the Dhofar Insurgency (1963-1975).

The host nation's involvement in the decision to build irregular forces is important from the beginning of the campaign. As the sole controller of state-sponsored violence, the host nation's government must decide how to restore order with national and local forces. In some cases, the use of national forces can exacerbate the problem by reinforcing the local populace's narrative.[13] Generally, the local populace identifies themselves as ethnically or culturally distinct from the majority of the national security force. The national government, with assistance from the interventionist power, must decide if a local force, with a similar identity, could address the unrest. The responsibility to build an irregular force could fall to the interventionist power.

Since World War II, the United States and the United Kingdom have typically served as interventionist powers and therefore assisted the host nation government with the creation of an irregular force. In current US Army and joint doctrine, security force assistance operations, specifically foreign internal defense, includes the training and partnership of indigenous security forces.[14] Since the early 1960s, Special Forces conducted the military component of this mission. However in post-September 11 operations, the US military quickly needed to expand their capability to conduct this mission in Iraq, Afghanistan, the Philippines and other locations during the War on Terror. In 2009, Secretary of Defense Robert Gates acknowledged the shortcoming when he wrote that "within the military, advising and mentoring indigenous security forces is moving from the periphery of institutional priorities, where it was considered the province of the Special Forces, to being a key mission for the armed forces as a whole."[15] However, in the UK, military capacity building and security sector reform doctrine addresses training of indigenous forces.[16] However, the UK Ministry of Defence lacks a unit dedicated to this mission.[17]

Whether or not an interventionist power decides to create a dedicated unit for this mission, effective partnership with regular and irregular security forces will remain a critical skill for the US and UK militaries. Partnership with locally raised security forces includes three overlapping techniques: training, mentoring, and observing.[18] All three techniques can exist simultaneously between the partnering unit and the indigenous force. Furthermore, the partnering unit could utilize one technique with the indigenous force's leadership, while employing a different component with the lower level Soldiers.

First, the partnering force provides training to the security forces during their formation. The formation period is often the most important since it establishes the relationship between the two forces. The partnering unit often works to establish discipline initially during the training component and when possible in ways reinforcing to the indigenous leadership structure. Both unit and personal discipline are important in a counterinsurgency and war in general. It ensures the unit is responsive to its leadership and it operates within the rule of law of the host nation. Discipline and legitimacy are linked traits. Furthermore, since the force is raised locally, grievances between the force and populace might factor into operations without partnership oversight. The training component is usually conducted away from the populace.

Second, the partnering force provides mentorship during the initial employment of the security forces. The indigenous force is capable of conducting simple operations independently, but often lack skilled refinement that results from multiple exposures to security operations. The advisors can physically lead the forces through its initial operations, or the advisors can indirectly lead the security forces by partnering with leaders.[19] The partnering force could also provide enablers not available to the local force including air support, indirect fire, and surveillance platforms.

Finally, the partnering unit provides observation of the indigenous force to ensure progress and legitimacy. Counterinsurgents seek an end state where is the local force is flexible, proficient, well led, and professional. It should operate among the populace and reinforce the government's rule of law. The interventionist power must hold the local force accountable throughout all phases of partnership, but accountability becomes more important as the interventionist power prepares to transition out of the host nation. Furthermore, the unit must be self-sustaining.[20] Both US and UK doctrine reinforce the fact that the process requires patience.

In addition to the method of partnership, another factor that differentiates the US and British experiences of raising indigenous security forces is the decision to reinforce or suppress tribal or ethnic differences when recruiting new Soldiers. Most advisors from the 19th and 20th centuries agreed that homogenous organizations preformed better than mixed units.[21] However, during the Cold War, the British and American emphasis on ethnic representation varied by insurgencies. In some cases, the American and British advisors tried both approaches with varying levels of success during the same campaign. Three case studies provide examples of varying levels of partnership and tribal or ethnic representation.

The Punjab Irregular Force, 1859-1886, and the later Frontier Corps from the early 20th century until 1947 is an example of a local security force formed with extensive partnership between British and indigenous leaders and with regard to differing tribal compositions in the 1850s. The British recruited Pashtuns, Sikhs, Gurkhas, and number of smaller classes to form the Punjab Irregular Force, also known as the "Piffers" to police the North-West Frontier. Unlike the development of later indigenous forces, the Piffers conducted internal security, not counterinsurgency operations.[22] Although organized as a paramilitary organization, the unit reported to the civil administrator, lieutenant governor of the Punjab, and not to the commander of British Indian Army. In British India, the army tended to assign British officers from the Indian Army to native regiments for the purposes of recruitment, training, discipline, and leadership.[23] British Indian Army officers partnered with native officers and noncommissioned officers to lead the Piffers. The British officers lived with their Soldiers, learned the language and the culture, and tended to represent the upper portion of British Indian officers. Later, Lord Curzon, then Viceroy of India, organized several local militias into the Frontier Corps. Although both the Piffers and the Frontier Corps participated in combat operations, they primarily provided internal security through the civil administrators.

The British involvement during the Dhofar Insurgency (1963-1975) provides examples of both successful and unsuccessful counterinsurgent creation of indigenous forces. In Dhofar, the Sultan's Armed Forces (SAF) fought against a communist-inspired and supported insurgency. The Special Air Service (SAS), under the moniker British Army Training Team (BATT), obtained permission from the Sultan to partner with local Dhofari tribes and build irregular units. After a period of trial and error, the BATT decided to reinforce the existing system of tribes and built tribally-based *firqats*. The BATT advisors to the *firqat* also represented a hand-selected group of officers and NCOs chosen specifically for their ability to accomplish the partnership task.

Finally, the Sons of Iraq (SoI) program in Baghdad and Al-Anbar province during Operation Iraqi Freedom demonstrates the creation of local indigenous force without regard for partnership. Sunni tribes in Al-Anbar province chose to side with the government instead of the insurgency in 2006 after three years of boycotting the government. Tribal leaders formed Sunni security forces to protect their neighborhoods and interests from Al-Qaeda extremists in order to gain relevance in national dialogue. American units in other parts of Iraq sought to mimic the success of local security forces in Al-Anbar province without the assistance of the

Awakening movement.[24] They created and financed SoI units at a rate that prevented partnership, standardization, and accountability. In the absence of guidance from the Iraqi government and Multi-National Forces-Iraq (MNF-I), SoI partnership with the Iraqi Ministry of Defense and the US military varied by the organization and the local US commander's personality. Without US partnership and consent of the Iraqi government, the SoI program initially lacked legitimacy as late as 2010.

American and British counterinsurgencies provide several case studies on the successful and unsuccessful creation of local irregular security forces. The paper examines the method of partnership, selection and traits of the advisors, and the host nation government's role in building the Punjab Irregular Force and Frontier Corps in the North-West Frontier in India, the *firqat* in Dhofar, and the Sons of Iraq. The paper discusses successful and unsuccessful practices for future counterinsurgents engaged in partnership missions with local irregular security forces. As the US and the UK consider their future force structures and their role as interventionist powers, "building partner capability", both regular and irregular, will remain relevant to current operations and future security assistance operations.

Notes

1.   Colonel Henry Lawrence served nearly his entire professional life as British Army officer and political agent in India. As an artillery officer, he participated in the First Burmese War, the First Afghan War, both Sikh Wars, and the Indian Mutiny. He advocated for the local populace as a political officer. He later served as the British Resident to the Darbar between the two Sikh wars. In this position, he also served as the chief political agent for the North-West Frontier. He proposed the formation of the Guides following the First Sikh War after observing the slow pace of the Indian Army regiments. Henry Lawrence died during the Siege of Lucknow in the Indian Mutiny of 1857. Lieutenant General James John McLeod Innes, *Sir Henry Lawrence: The Pacificator* (Oxford: Clarendon Press, 1898), 11-16.

2.   US Army doctrine defines irregular forces as "armed individuals or groups who are not members of the regular armed forces, police, or other internal security forces." Despite the fact that this term is part of the doctrinal lexicon, the term is most often used to only describe the enemy insurgents. Irregular forces are also called auxiliaries, militias, and local security forces. Department of the Army, Field Manual 1-02 *Operational Terms and Graphics* s.v. "Irregular Forces" (Washington, DC: Government Printing Office, 21 September 2004), 1-105.

3.   *History of the Guides, 1846-1922* (Aldershot: Gale and Polden, 1938), 2-3.

4.   Military Training Team (MiTT) training for the US was centralized at Fort Riley on 1 June 2006 to standardize the training teams received prior to deploying to Iraq. First Brigade, 1st Infantry Division received responsibility for training the teams. The unit received the first Afghanistan MiTTs in November 2006. Prior to that time, advisors received training in one of four locations. The Iraq Study Group found that the advisory mission was critically understaffed in 2006. The group cited a target number of 10,000-20,000 advisors for Iraq; however, the US military had only 3,000-4,000 in place. James A. Baker, III and Lee H. Hamilton, eds., *The Iraq Study Group Report: The Way Forward –A New Approach* (New York: Vintage, 2006), 70-71. The UK did not form Training Teams until *Operation Charge of the Knights* in Basra, March 2008. Daniel Marston, "Adaptation in the Field: The British Army's Difficult Campaign in Iraq," *Security Challenges* 6, no. 1 (Autumn 2010): 78-81.

5.   FM 3-24 *Counterinsurgency* superseded FM 7-98 *Operations in Low Intensity Conflict* (1992) and FM 90-8 *Counterguerrilla Operations* (1986). Neither manual devoted space to the training of regular or irregular security forces since Special Forces traditionally conducted this mission. FM 90-8 did encourage commanders to partner with host nation forces whenever possible. The authors also devoted four paragraphs in the last appendix stating that US Army forces could perform advisory missions with paramilitary and irregular forces to train locally recruited forces for local defense missions. No other guidance is provided. Even the interim counterinsurgency manual, FMI 3-07.22,

Counterinsurgency Operations, 1 October 2006, lacked guidance concerning advisory and partnership missions. Department of the Army, Field Manual 90-8 *Counterguerrilla Operations* (Washington, DC: Government Printing Office, 29 August 1986), H-14–H-16.

6.   This is only a partial list of irregular forces used by the US and the UK. Not all of these case studies are explained in detail in this paper. The Punjab and Dhofar are explained in detail in Chapter 3 and Chapter 4 of this paper. In South Africa, the British co-opted nearly 2,000 Boers for service in the South African Constabulary, as well as other irregular formations. See Byron Farwell, *The Great Boer War* (New York: Harper and Row, 1976). In the Philippines, the US Army built the Philippine Constabulary and the Philippine Scouts. See Brian Linn, *The Philippine War, 1899-1902* (Lawrence: University of Kansas Press, 2000) and Alfred McCoy, *Policing America's Empire* (Madison, WI:University of Wisconsin Press, 2009), 82-93, 126-146 for more details on the Philippine irregular forces. The British and Malayans formed the Home Guard from Chinese immigrants during the Malayan Emergency. James Corum, *Training Indigenous Forces in Counterinsurgency: A Tale of Two Insurgencies* (Carlisle: Strategic Studies Institute, March 2006), 1-24 and 34-54. In Vietnam, the US mentored the Montagnards in the Vietnamese Central Highlands. See Lieutenant Colonel Lewis Burruss, *Mike Force* (Lincoln: Pocketbooks, 1989) for a first-person account of training and operating with the Montagnard tribesmen. Finally, the US partnered with the Kurdish Peshmerga, the Sons of Iraq (Concerned Local Citizens), and 3rd Battalion, 6th Marine Regiment's partnership with the Albu Mahal tribe in Al Qa'im. See Carter Malkasian, "Counterinsurgency in Iraq," in *Counterinsurgency in Modern Warfare*, ed. Daniel Marston and Carter Malkasian (Oxford: Osprey Publishing, 2010), 287-310.

7.   The US Army defines population control as "determining who lives in an area and what they do." Population control is discussed further in Chapter 2. Department of the Army, Field Manual 3-24 *Counterinsurgency* (Chicago: University of Chicago Press, 2007), 180.

8.   *History of the Guides, 1846-1922*, 2-3; Innes, 27.

9.   Partnership is not defined in US Army or joint doctrine. The closest doctrinal term is security force assistance, which is "the unified action to generate, employ, and sustain local, Host Nation, or regional security forces in support of a legitimate authority." Department of the Army, Field Manual 3-07 *Stability Operations* (Ann Arbor: University of Michigan Press, 2009), 6-77. However, this definition does not translate well to tactical units for implementation. General David Petraeus did not provide a definition in his COIN guidance to commanders during surge operations in Iraq. General Stanley McChrystal's "ISAF Commander's Counterinsurgency Guidance" provides one of the best tactical-level definitions of partnership. He wrote, "live, eat, and train together, plan and operate together, depend on one another, and hold each other accountable–at all echelons down to the Soldier level. Treat them as equal partners in success." Headquarters,

International Security Assistance Force "ISAF Commander's Counterinsurgency Guidance" (Kabul, 25 August 2009), 7. General Petraeus kept the same words in commander's guidance as the ISAF Commander.

10. *History of the Guides, 1846-1922,* 3.

11. Hans J. Morgenthau, *Politics Among Nations: The Struggle for Power and Peace,* 7th ed. (New York: McGraw-Hill, 2006), 284.

12. The US advisory mission to the Montagnards in Vietnam suffered from this problem. Military Assistance Command-Vietnam failed to vet the program through the South Vietnamese government. As a result, the Civilian Irregular Defense Group (CIDG) and later MIKE Force units received no funding or material from the Vietnamese government. In 1970, the US abandoned the program during the Vietnamization program. Burress, 190. It remains to be seen if the Government of Iraq will fully integrate the Sons of Iraq into the government's forces.

13. An example of this problem is explained in Chapter 4. Although not a case study in this paper, another example of this paradox is the use of India's military in Indian-administered Kashmir. Although the conflict is rooted within the larger problems of the partition of India and Pakistan in 1947, the Kashmiris are predominately Muslim. However, India is predominately Hindu. Additionally, the Kashmiris believe that the Armed Forces (Jammu and Kashmir) Special Powers Act passed in 1990 unfairly allows the military forces to discriminate against them. See Sumantra Rose's *Kashmir: Roots of Conflict, Paths to Peace* (Cambridge: Harvard University Press: 2005); Sumit Ganguly "Explaining the Kashmir Insurgency: Political Mobilization and Institutional Decay," *International Security* 21, no. 2 (Autumn 1996): 76-107; Ashutosh Varshney, "India, Pakistan, and Kashmir: Antimonies of Nationalism," *Asian Survey* 31, no. 11 (November 1991): 997-1019 for more information on the role of paramilitary forces in the Kashmir insurgency.

14. Foreign internal defense (FID) is "the participation by civilian and military agencies of a government in any of the action programs taken by another government or other designated organization, to free and protect its society from subversion, lawlessness, insurgency, terrorism, and other threats to their security." FID is divided into categories, indirect and direct. Indirect FID focuses on systems in the target nation and includes military exchange programs, and joint and multinational exercises. Direct FID is usually conducted US Special Forces and includes the use of US forces normally focused on civil-military operations, psychological operations (PSYOP), communications and intelligence cooperation, mobility, and logistic support. Department of the Army, Field Manual 3-07.1 *Security Force Assistance* (Washington, DC: Government Printing Office, 1 May 2009), 1-4, paragraph 1-25; Department of Defense, Joint Publication 3-22 *Foreign Internal Defense* (Washington, DC: Government Printing Office, 12 July 2010), ix-x.

15. Robert M. Gates "Helping Others Defend Themselves: The Future of US Security Assistance," *Foreign Affairs* (May/June 2010): 2.

16. Military Capacity Building describes the range of activities in support of developing an indigenous security force including partnering, monitoring, mentoring, and training. Security Sector Reform is a specific program of activities coordinated to create capable indigenous security forces (police and armed forces) generally tailored to a specific theatre. Ministry of Defence, British Army Field Manual Volume 1 Part 10 *Countering Insurgency* (London: Ministry of Defence, October 2009), 10-1, 10-B-3.

17. The issue of training a unit specifically for partnership missions remains a contentious issue in both countries. There are advantages and disadvantages to creating dedicated group of advisors. Potential advantages include specialization of the Soldiers for this type of mission, protected career progression, and education tailored for this type of mission. The primary disadvantage of specialization is the inability to use these Soldiers for other missions, a key criteria as both countries are getting ready to decrease the end strength of the military. See Center for Technology and National Security Policy, *Transforming for Stabilization and Reconstruction Operations* (Washington, DC: National Defense University, 12 November 2003); Edward F. Bruner, *Military Forces: What is the Appropriate Size for the United States?* (Washington, DC: Congressional Research Service, 10 February 2005) for more information on the US debate.

18. The terms partnering, mentoring, and advising appear prominently in several documents related to past and present insurgencies, including the mission statements of both training commands in Iraq and Afghanistan, but remain for the most part undefined in American doctrine. The terms are discussed, but not defined, in Chapter 8, FM 3-24.2, *Tactics in Counterinsurgency*. Conversely, British doctrine uses the term M2T (monitor, mentor, and train) to describe a spectrum of military support to indigenous forces during the transition or building phase. Partnership is described as an end state when both forces are equal and integrated. *Countering Insurgency*, 10-A-1, paragraphs 10-A-3 and 10-A-4. In order to establish a common language for the purposes of this discussion, partnership simply refers to the relationship between the counterinsurgent and the local force during the formation of the unit.

19. This aspect is discussed within the context of each case study presented. The US's preferred method currently is indirect. In the US, the national command authority must authorize the potential involvement of military personnel in combat operations with indigenous forces. If at all possible, the advisors should use every opportunity to reinforce the local force leadership. When problems present during operations, the advisor should avoid discrediting the indigenous force leaders in front of subordinates.

20. Department of the Army, *Counterinsurgency*, 208.

21. Commentators on this subject fail to reach agreement. Lieutenant General Sir Harry Lumsden, who commanded the Guides in the North-West

Frontier Province, offered advice on the matter in "Frontier Thoughts and Frontier Requirements." He recommended the creation of regiments based on race or nationality as method of building loyalty and *esprit de corps*. However, he encouraged recruiting from every caste to build these units. Segregation of the castes by company within the regiment was "convenient." His recommendation disagreed with the common practice following the Mutiny in 1857. T. E. Lawrence also concluded that tribal and ethnic composition was important. He included it his advisory piece "Twenty-Seven Articles" and commented that he had never seen a successful operation that mixed Bedu and Syrians, but had witnessed many failures. For the Americans, the recruitment of indigenous forces almost always followed tribal or ethnic lines. In the American West, General George Crook recruited several organizations of Native American axillaries, often exploiting divisions with a tribe. General Order 293 established the fifty companies of Scouts by tribe or language group during the Philippine Insurrection. See Sir Harry Lumsden, *Lumsden of the Guides* (London: John Murray, 1899), Appendix A, 291-292; T. E. Lawrence, "Twenty-Seven Articles," *The Arab Bulletin* (20 August 1917): Article 15; Alfred McCoy, *Policing America's Empire* (Madison: University of Wisconsin Press, 2009), 83; Robert M. Utley, *Frontier Regulars: The United States Army and the Indian, 1866-1891* (Lincoln: University of Nebraska Press, 1973), 53-57.

22. The Piffers conducted a mission known formally as aid to the civil power that included punishing and rewarding tribes, escorting civil authorities, and guarding British interests from the raiders. The distinction between aid to the civil power and counterinsurgency is described in chapter 2.

23. This system differed from the more common, and later, practice of seconded British officers to other armies. Seconding an officer involves releasing the officer for set period of time from his assigned unit to another, usually native, unit. When the assignment is complete the officer returns to assigned unit.

24. The Anbar Awakening and the Sons of Iraq program are different aspects of the Sunni Awakening. The Anbar Awakening was a grassroots initiative started by Sunni tribal leaders, specifically Sheikh Abdul Sattar Abu Risha. The Iraqi government and US military supported the initiative and provided some material support. General David Petraeus started the SoI program to spread the success of the Anbar Awakening to other Sunni areas. Najim Abed Al-Jabouri and Sterling Jensen, "The Iraqi and AQI roles in the Sunni Awakening," *Prism* 2, no. 1 (December 2010): 3-4.

Chapter 2
Theory

A commander can more easily shape and direct the popular insurrection by supporting the insurgents with small units of the regular army. Without these regular troops to provide encouragement, the local inhabitants will usually lack the confidence and initiative to take arms.

- Carl von Clausewitz, *On War*

Although the topic of raising local irregular security forces gained attention during the Iraq War surge, as Colonel Lawrence alluded to in his letter to the Governor-General in the previous chapter, the use of these forces is not a new idea. In fact, he considered the use of local irregular forces to assist the civil government self-apparent in June 1846. The theory and practice of using the local population to supplement an imperial, governmental, or counterinsurgent power dates to at the least the early Roman Empire, if not earlier.[1] Carl von Clausewitz's writings on the nature of war help provide the theoretical foundation to explain the importance of the indigenous population's involvement in waging war. His theory postulated that the populace's relationship with the government and the military is important when waging a war. Several contemporary theorists, including Mao Tse-tung, Frank Kitson, and David Galula, reinforced Clausewitz's work as it applied to the post-World War II period to further explain the importance of population security.[2] These authors developed their theories when fighting revolutionary wars, or wars of national liberation, was especially prevalent.[3]

Before commencing any discussion on the relationships between the government, military, and the populace, it is important to define war. Carl von Clausewitz's collection of books, *On War*, provided both classical and contemporary theorists with one definition of war. He stated war was an act of organized violence to compel the enemy to do your will.[4] His statement is decidedly vague and allows the counterinsurgent and the host nation government a wide variety of options short of armed conflict. These include but are not limited to negotiation, appeal to international organizations, and economic sanctions.

Once a host nation decides that to wage war, it must decide what type of war to wage. Clausewitz briefly divides war into two broad categories, total and limited war. He described the first category, total war, as a desire to overthrow the enemy, either by rendering him politically or militarily ineffective. Limited war sought to occupy an objective long enough to secure an advantageous position, either physically or diplomatically.[5] In wars of national liberation, the local population and the government might be fighting each other with different objectives. The populace could fight using a total war mindset, while the counterinsurgent is fighting a limited war.[6] Furthermore, the indigenous host nation's government and the interventionist power could also be fighting different levels of war.[7]

A nation at war needs to balance the interactions between the government, the military, and the populace. War is a function of the relationship between the three elements, primordial violence, probability, and policy. Clausewitz referred to these relationships as the paradoxical trinity.[8] How the three elements interact with each other is just as important to understanding insurgencies and counterinsurgencies, as is the definition of war. Clausewitz stated that populace is the primary means of expression for the primordial violence, or passion, piece of the relationship. The military commander and his army are responsible for chance and probability. Finally, the government is the sole actor when concerned with policy.[9]

Although most politicians and military professionals understand the importance of a balanced civil-military relationship, the interaction of the populace with the military and government are not always considered when conducting a war. Recruiting and parades are examples of the populace-military interaction, whereas war bond drives, taxes, and the Selective Service Act are examples of populace-government interactions.

The government must decide how much to involve the populace in the conduct of the war. Clausewitz stated that the people's passion for war must be present when the conflict started. However, the government might seek to manipulate the passion once the war is started. In one of President George W. Bush's first speeches following the 11 September 2001 attacks on the World Trade Center and the Pentagon he tried to reduce the public's passion for immediate reprisals.[10] During the 1968 Presidential campaign, Richard Nixon had to address the growing dissatisfaction with the Vietnam War because of a vocal group of American citizens.[11] Finally, the government might also decide to control the interaction between the populace and the military. For example, a state might use the military to institute martial law to quell the populace's passion for a particular cause and to increase the military's probability of victory through the use of population control measures.[12]

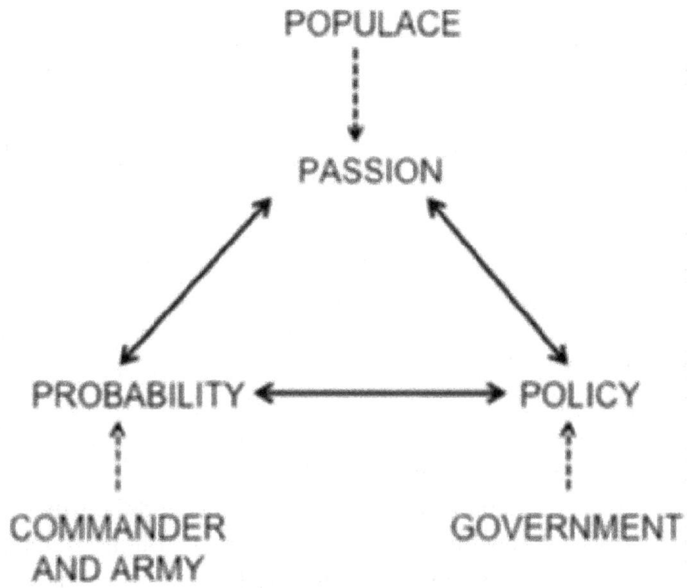

POPULACE

PASSION

PROBABILITY ←————————→ POLICY

COMMANDER
AND ARMY   GOVERNMENT

Figure 1. Clausewitz's Paradoxical Trinity with their Actors.
Source: Created by author.

By examining the relationships between the three elements of the paradoxical trinity and their primary actors, it is easier to understand why Clausewitz believed that war was a continuation of policy by another means.[13] This statement is important to any discussion of insurgency and counterinsurgency because the local population's relationship with the military and the government. Although Clausewitz did not expand his thoughts beyond a few sentences on the matter, several contemporary theorists wrote about the importance of the population during an insurgency. Mao Tse-Tung, for example, believed that revolutionary warfare was necessary to address societal grievances, whether they are equal voting rights, land ownership, or the freedom of assembly. The populace could seek redress through warfare for these perceived wrongs.[14] Over time, the people's grievances can inflame their passion for change. Sir Robert Thompson captured this lesson in his counterinsurgency theory. He stated that every insurgency required a cause, generally based on a real or believed social gap between the people and the government.[15]

Often the government or counterinsurgent often has to address these perceived causes as part of their strategy. Clausewitz's idea of ways, ends, and means is one method of examining the problem confronting the counterinsurgent. Clausewitz explained the ways, ends, and means at both the strategic and tactical levels of war, although it is primarily at the strategic level that it is important to discuss of the peoples' role. Clausewitz explained that armies, through a series of victories, provide the strategic means, while the government provides the ends by determining the peace objectives at the end of the conflict.[16] Clausewitz left the reader to infer that the people provide the ways for war conducted through their support of the war, both material and moral.

The Dhofar Insurgency is an example of the ways, ends, and means applied to a populace to solve a strategic problem. The Sultan's Armed Forces (SAF) lacked intelligence on the insurgents operating in Dhofar, and therefore they lacked the ability to meaningfully attack the enemy. The Sultan defined the strategic ends as defeating the insurgency, while maintaining sovereignty over the Dhofar region. He co-opted the Dhofari tribes; a group previously discriminated against by the previous Sultan, as one of the ways to achieve his end state. He allowed the tribes to form their own security forces to gather intelligence, patrol, and fight against the insurgents. Eventually, the SAF and the Dhofari tribes defeated the insurgents through a series of military campaigns (the means). The Sultan also influenced the relationship between the populace and the government by instituting a series of social reforms in Dhofar to address the Dhofaris' social grievances.[17]

The Dhofar example also demonstrates that another important aspect of counterinsurgency, the "whole of government" approach to the problem. British General Frank Kitson advised future counterinsurgents that a purely military solution does not exist for an insurgency. He postulated that the military campaign must work within an overall government plan that also included political and economic solutions. The plan needed to address the insurgents' aims, strengths, and weaknesses.[18] David Galula continued this theme to an extreme and stated that depriving the insurgency of the cause solves the problem of an insurgency.[19] However, the government does not need to capitulate to the insurgents' demands. Kitson understood that the government and counterinsurgent needed to balance force and incentives when dealing with the populace. Until the Malaya Emergency ended in 1960, the Malayan government, advised by the British, never allowed the Chinese immigrants living in the country full rights, including universal citizenship and proportional representation in the national government, but they did address several of discriminatory practices that prevented them from making a fair living.[20]

The paradoxical trinity and the ways, ends, and means analysis also help explain the basis of population control theory. Counterinsurgency

(COIN) practitioners tend to avoid the term population control when developing operations since control of the population often conflicts with their liberal democratic values.[21] The US Army defines population control as "determining who lives in an area and what they do."[22] Population control measures include the use of curfews, movement restrictions, censuses, registration cards, and the forced resettlement of villagers.[23] Furthermore, population control measures often attempt to balance two competing principles of counterinsurgency operations. First, the counterinsurgent forces must try to isolate the populace from the insurgent to prevent insurgent recruitment, indoctrination, and material support from the populace. A counterinsurgent can use physical, coercive, and incentive-based means to achieve physical and psychological isolation between the insurgent and the local populace. Simultaneously, the counterinsurgent forces, both as the host nation as well as the interventionist power, must convince the populace of the legitimacy of its position to defeat an insurgency and reinforce the primacy of government's rule of law.

The government's use of population control can easily disrupt the relationships between the people, government, and the army. Clausewitz likened this relationship to the balance between three magnets, passion, policy, and probability.[24] When the equilibrium between the three magnets is disrupted, a state of internal unrest can exist. Likewise, if the people do not provide the ways for war, the government or the army might seek to control public sentiment by imposing taxes, martial law, conscription, and rationing. General insurrection by the people exists on Clausewitz's spectrum of war when something disrupts the relationship between the populace and the government. Clausewitz acknowledged in "The People in Arms" that general insurrection is defeated slowly by removing the passion for uprising from the people.[25] Population control measures seek to manipulate the people's passion by isolating the insurgent. It is not necessary to co-opt the populace initially to guarantee success (initially the measure could be coercive in nature).

Not all contemporary theorists agree on the relative importance of the populace when waging war. In fact, British General Rupert Smith, a contemporary theorist, argued that the populace's passion for war is the least important factor for sustaining a state of war. However, it must be present.[26] Although Smith cites several examples of counterinsurgencies in attempt to substantiate his equation in terms of political will, he fails to discuss the importance of the popular opinion. Vietnam is an example where he claimed the US lost the will to fight politically, but he fails to mention the importance of the anti-war movement in the country at the time.[27] In fact, his mathematical reduction of Clausewitz's theory of war underestimates the importance of the people in insurgency and counterinsurgency warfare. While his error in overlooking Clausewitz's chapter on people's war is perhaps excusable, he completely ignored the writings of Mao Tse-Tung.

Mao Tse-Tung's theories on the nature of revolutionary warfare stress the importance of the populace for sustaining war. His writings bridge the classical period to the contemporary period. His book, *On Guerrilla Warfare*, describes the tenets of peoples' wars that influenced an entire generation of counterinsurgency theorists. Mao reiterated Clausewitz's theories by describing why the populace is important to the insurgent in revolutionary warfare. Mao suggested that the insurgency must exploit perceived societal gaps between the government and the populace.[28] In theory, the insurgent can also deal with the populace using the same physical, coercive, and incentive-based means as the counterinsurgent. The average villager only needs to believe that the insurgent can give him a better life than the government for the counterinsurgent to start losing the battle for the populace's minds.

While Mao wrote from insurgent's viewpoint, Galula emphasized the importance of winning the fight for the populace for the counterinsurgent. His theory further divided Clausewitz's interactions between the populace, state, and military by framing the insurgency in terms of military, political, and social issues. Galula's first principle for counterinsurgency operations stated that the aim of the war is to gain support of the population, not the application of violence to control territory.[29] In fact, he believed that gaining and maintaining contact with the population is a major theme of the ideal counterinsurgency operation.[30] Over time, this emphasis on the population has supported the so-called "population-centric" model of counterinsurgency.[31]

Since the insurgent and the counterinsurgent are competing for the support of the populace, the government and interventionist power must develop a plan to exploit their strengths. Often times, the government has relative advantages in resources including money, military strength, and infrastructure. Sir Robert Thompson developed five principles to defeating a communist insurgency based on his experience in Malaya. These principles emphasize the legitimacy and transparency of the government as necessary to isolate the populace and defeat the insurgency. The first principle is the government needed a clear political goal.[32] Every contemporary theorist echoes this principle, and Thompson's assessment reinforces Clausewitz's assertion that the political objective of war is the

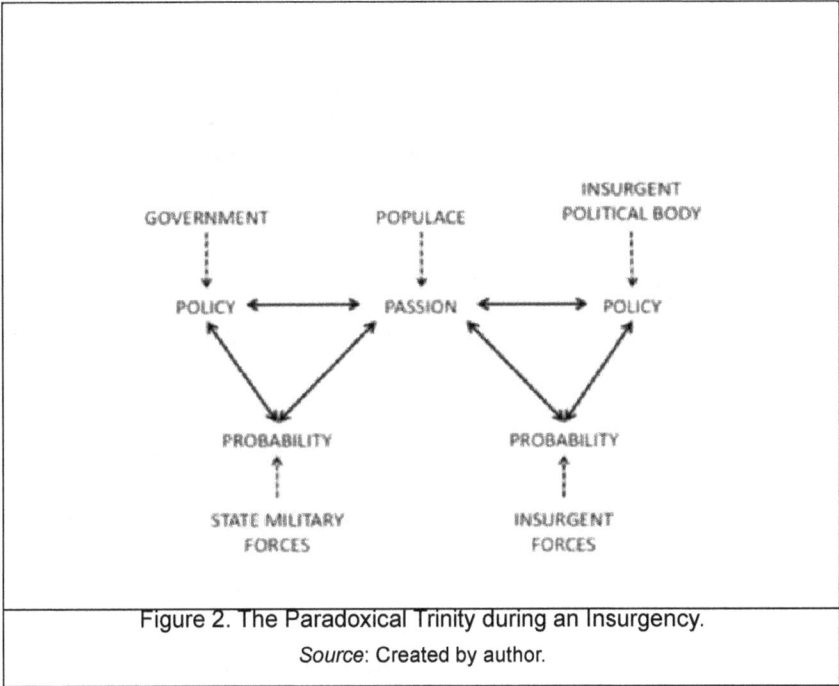

Figure 2. The Paradoxical Trinity during an Insurgency.
Source: Created by author.

most important. The second principle is the legitimacy of government's strategy. Third, the government must have an overall plan. The fourth principle is the government must defeat the political subversion, not the insurgent force. Finally, the government must secure base areas first.[33] The last two principles seek to physically and psychologically isolate the population from the insurgents. Additionally, the government must defeat subversion by removing the issues that the population perceives is at issue when possible. Although these principles do not specifically state that the population should be actively involved in the strategy, the counterinsurgent could conclude to use the population to secure its base areas as part of their ways, ends, and means analysis.

The Rationale for Indigenous Security Forces

The application of Clausewitz's and Mao's theories on war to Thompson's fifth principle helps provide the rationale for creating local security forces. Mao stressed the population's inclusion developing ways, ends, and means for fighting a war. Given the importance of the population during an insurgency, the counterinsurgent should also place emphasis on the population. The counterinsurgent can use the local populace to help secure base areas. Contemporary theorists including Kitson and Galula agree that the counterinsurgent and host nation government must gain a quick victory to demonstrate their resolve. Kitson argued that the main characteristic, which distinguished insurgency from other forms of war, is the struggle for men's minds with violence used to support or perpetuate ideas.[34] If the counterinsurgent can convince the populace to actively secure their interests, without fear of insurgent reprisal, then the counterinsurgent is starting to win the information battle.

However, the populace is rarely able to secure itself against terrorism at the beginning of an insurgency. Kitson used the case studies in *Bunch of Five* to demonstrate this paradox and the problems it created when developing the counterinsurgent's overall plan.[35] The military initially provided local security in each case. Thompson stated that a counterinsurgent wanted to quickly create the conditions where individuals needed to pick between supporting the government and the insurgent. The counterinsurgent should allow the population to secure itself using local paramilitary forces because it could influence the population to support the government.[36] Mao suggested that units from the home province could provide the local security, a point that several contemporary theorists echoed.[37]

During the wars in Iraq and Afghanistan, David Kilcullen examined importance of local security forces in both theory and doctrine from an interventionist perspective. As part of his statement of best counterinsurgency practices, he added the tenet, "Effective, Legitimate Local Security Forces." He viewed these forces in the same manner as Kitson, guards that allowed better-trained Soldiers to conduct offensive missions. He added some important criteria to his description of the local force; legitimate in the local eyes, operate under the rule of law, and can effectively protect local communities against insurgents. He also added a word of caution for the interventionist power: the formation and training of these troops takes more time and resources than is usually appreciated.[38]

If the counterinsurgent decides to form of irregular units, they can also assist the counterinsurgent with the gathering of information. Almost all of the other contemporary counterinsurgent theorists agree that the role of intelligence is paramount to conducting a successful counterinsurgency.[39] The gathering of intelligence is another argument for the creation of indigenous security forces. Trinquier notes that a paradox exists for the counterinsurgent, in that intelligence gathering is paramount to conducting offensive operations, but the population is generally reluctant to share information with the counterinsurgent.[40] The population could fear reprisals from insurgent forces, be subject to enemy propaganda, or view the security forces as part of the real or perceived societal issue.

It is important to note that the building of indigenous security forces is not limited to counterinsurgency campaigns. In fact, the majority of local security forces are trained for internal security or policing duties. British Major General Sir Charles Gwynn stated in *Imperial Policing* that the army provides an important role in the maintenance of law and order.[41] Although Gwynn's book presents case studies from Imperial Britain, its relevance to modern campaigns should not be dismissed as a relic of an earlier era. Gwynn believed then that the army's policing functions were increasing in importance to its wartime duties. He divided policing duties into three categories. The first category included small wars, campaigns with a limited, defined military objective.[42] This category included punitive campaigns. Gwynn chose to emphasize the second category, which consisted of campaigns where civil control of the population does not exist, or has broken down to the extent where the military is the only institution that can provide security. The United States Army conducted this type of campaign following the fall of Baghdad in March 2003 until the restoration of Iraqi national sovereignty on 28 June 2004. A unique feature of this type of campaign is the divided responsibility between the military and civil authorities. The third category is a campaign where the civil government maintains control, but lacks the personnel numbers to provide adequate security for the populace.[43] Examples of this type of campaign are the current wars in Afghanistan and Iraq.

The British military published a series of manuals to help leaders understand how their responsibilities and powers changed in this type of campaign. In 1949, British doctrine defined this type of military operation as "in aid of the civil power to restore law and order."[44] Over time, the name given to these operations changed several times, but the subordinate tasks remained fairly constant. In the 1957 and 1963 versions of the manual, this term evolved into the range of tasks known as internal security.[45] Derivatives of these manuals and internal security tasks eventually formed the core of British Army's 1977 Counter Revolutionary Operations manual, which was published following the decolonization of the Empire east of the Suez Canal. It continued to address the role of British forces fighting primarily against communist insurgencies.[46] The evolution of British doctrine is important to understanding how the raising of indigenous security forces in the Empire influenced later campaigns. The US Army also codified the levels of policing and their relation to war fighting in the counterinsurgency field manual, FM 3-24.[47]

Force Ratios

In the current international environment of constrained budgets, recession, and limited military interventions, theorists have reopened the discussion of whether a certain number or ratio of troops are needed to counter an insurgency. The idea of force ratios warrants examination in the discussion whether or not to raise indigenous local security forces. Force ratios are defined one of two ways. The force ratio can define the relative strength in numbers of insurgents to counterinsurgents, or counterinsurgents to the population.[48]

The force ratio number seems to lack scientific validity, even though the US has used this as a metric since the 1980s.[49] Further studies in the 1990s perpetuated this force ratio.[50] Leading up to the war in Iraq, senior defense officials argued about the number of troops needed to stabilize Iraq immediately following the invasion. This debate reached its climax when General Eric Shinseki testified to the Senate Armed Forces Committee that several hundred thousand troops were needed.[51] In 2007, General David Petraeus included the ratio in the interim FMI 3-07-22.[52] The Field Manual 3-24, *Counterinsurgency*, suggested a force density of 20 counterinsurgents per 1,000 people as a minimum and a ratio of 25 to 1,000 as a maximum.[53] The Institute for Defense Analyses found that force density of 40-50 counterinsurgents per 1,000 is required for high confidence of success.[54] The researchers limited the scope of their analysis to Iraq, and to a lesser extent Afghanistan, Bosnia, and Kosovo.[55] The study recommended a revision of *Counterinsurgency* to reflect their results.[56] However, other studies have demonstrated that ratios of 1.3:1 in the Philippines and 4:1 in El Salvador produced counterinsurgency wins.[57] In Iraq, the best ratio that the government and coalition troops achieved was 18.4:1 at the beginning of 2007.[58] At best, these studies demonstrate that using case studies does not conclusively prove the 10:1 ratio or even the 20:1 ratio. The studies reinforce Kitson's statement that military force at a certain level alone cannot produce a counterinsurgent win. Instead, the studies on force ratios allude to the fact that the military component is only one aspect of a complex problem that requires Thompson's "whole of government" approach to produce a victory.

Some of the contemporary theorists have suggested that the inclusion of irregular Soldiers to change the force ratio is valid, not necessarily for the numbers, but instead because they allow regular Soldiers to conduct more missions that require more skill sets. Kitson's argument for the creation of auxiliaries focused on the manpower requirements of his "framework operations," specifically the defensive operations. He suggested that auxiliary forces could assume less skilled tasks such as guarding and protection.[59] In turn, the use of auxiliaries for guarding and protection tasks allowed the army and police to conduct offensive operations, intelligence gathering, and information operations. Kitson also noted that by co-opting a neutral population to conduct local security operations that it could have the unintended effect of forcing that person to join the side of the government.[60] Trinquier developed a similar conclusion, but also stated that any member of the population supporting the counterinsurgent deprives the insurgent of material, information, and sanctuary.[61]

Thompson provided a less utilitarian explanation than Trinquier or Kitson; however, it is perhaps the best argument against a fixed force ratio. He argued in *Defeating Communist Insurgency* that force ratios are irrelevant when fighting a counterinsurgency due to the number of variables that a belligerent must consider. First, the counterinsurgent needs to take into account the insurgent's organization. Second, the terrain is an important factor to consider. Third, the counterinsurgent needs to consider the relationships between the different security organizations and the relationship with the host government.[62] Exact force ratios are not as important as the counterinsurgent's relative rate of increase or decrease to the insurgent's. In other words, an improving trend over time is more important than attaining a certain ratio of ten counterinsurgents to every one insurgent.[63]

The creation of the Philippine Constabulary in July 1901 is a historical example of Thompson's idea on force ratios. In July 1901, the United States transitioned the Philippines from the military authority to civilian authority. The departure of all US Volunteer Soldiers from the Philippines coincided with that transition. The redeployment of the Volunteer regiments would have changed the force ratio in the Philippines significantly in favor of the insurgents. Since, the US Volunteer regiments comprised about 50-percent of the US Army's fighting strength in the Philippines, or about 35,000 Soldiers.[64] Major General Arthur MacArthur proposed creating a small native force to fill the gap left by the departing volunteers. The Taft government created the Philippine Constabulary in July 1901 and Philippine Scouts in September 1901.[65] One year after their creation, the scouts and constabulary comprised 40-percent of the counterinsurgent force, or about 11,000 men. The number of insurgents also decreased proportionally during the same time period due to a number of reasons including on-going pacification campaigns by the US Army and the native irregulars and further disillusionment with the insurgency following Aguinaldo's capture in March 1901. By July 1905 the number of native irregulars had increased to 21,000.[66] However, Linn concludes that if the US followed the prevailing theory on force ratios between insurgents and counterinsurgents, than the US Army would have required a force of 80,000-100,000 regulars and several tens of thousands auxiliaries. Instead, the peak strength of US involvement reached 70,000 Soldiers, and averaged about 42,000.[67] The increasing or stable of trend of counterinsurgents to insurgents allowed for an eventual counterinsurgency success.

In conclusion, Clausewitz's and Mao's theories, combined with more contemporary theorists, demonstrate the importance of the population when developing a counterinsurgency campaign. The government and military must achieve balance with the population by addressing perceived societal gaps. One method of focusing on the populace's passion for the host nation's war is to allow, or even to provide assistance for the creation of local irregular security forces. By allowing their creation, the government and the military increase their relationships with the populace. Finally, the creation of local security forces increases the number of counterinsurgents relative to the number of insurgents, which allows the counterinsurgent force to use better-trained Soldiers for offensive operations.

Notes

1.   This study is primarily concerned with the raising of auxiliaries in the 20th and 21st centuries. See Edward Luttwak, *Grand Strategy of the Roman Empire* for a discussion of how the Roman Empire used local auxiliaries to provide security and Vegetius's *De Re Militari* for discussions of the uses and employment of auxiliaries. The United States also developed auxiliary units to fight in its wars. John Tierney Jr.'s earlier chapters in *Chasing Ghosts: Unconventional Warfare in American History* quickly describe the use of auxiliaries in the period of the Revolutionary War through the American Civil War. Robert Utley discussed the brief use of tribes during post-Civil War period in *Frontier Regulars: The United States Army and the Indian, 1866-1891.*

2.   This study uses the terms classical and contemporary to describe theorists and their works. The classical period includes all writing on the subject of warfare and the use of auxiliaries through the end of the Second World War. The contemporary period includes the post-1945 writings until the present day. The distinction is perhaps artificial and corresponds only due to the appearance of the term revolutionary warfare in military lexicon to describe wars of decolonization that counterinsurgents thought were inspired by Mao the worldwide communist movement. Some contemporary theorists argue that a third period, the post-Maoist period should be used to describe the current wars in Iraq and Afghanistan. See John Mackinlay's *Insurgent Archipelago* for description of the post-Maoist counterinsurgency.

3.   "Wars of national liberation" is a Marxist term for a conflict when an oppressed minority fights against an imperial power. They are also referred to as wars of independence. Western counterinsurgents referred to them revolutionary wars.

4.   Carl von Clausewitz, *On War*, trans. and ed. Michael Howard and Peter Paret (Princeton, NJ: Princeton University Press, 1976), 75.

5.   Clausewitz., 69. Limited war also includes military actions where the belligerents may not come into direct contact such as blockades, no-fly zones, drone strikes, and cyber warfare.

6.   An example of this scenario occurred in Yugoslavia during World War II in German-occupied Europe. The German *Wehrmacht* and police confronted numerous partisan movements in occupied France, Soviet Union, and Eastern Europe. The Germans could not spare the manpower to fight an all-out offensive against the partisans. As a result, the German occupation forces often fought limited offensives designed to cripple, but not destroy, the partisan movements. The German government had to balance their tactics with the desired end state in each region. In the Ukraine, the Germans depopulated entire regions to prevent resistance movements, but in France they assumed a more benevolent approach to the population. However, in each case the partisans continued to fight the Germans using all tactics available to them. See Peter Lieb, "Few Carrots and a

lot of Sticks," in *Counterinsurgency in Modern Warfare,* ed. Daniel Marston and Carter Malkasian (Oxford: Osprey Publishing, 2010), 57-77.

7.   The recent conflict in Libya is an example of this situation. NATO conducted a limited war in support of the National Transition Council, which most NATO countries recognized as the legitimate government during the campaign. While Libyan rebels were fighting to destroy the Muammar Gaddafi government, NATO only participated on the fringes providing a naval blockade, bombing limited targets, and enforcing a no-fly zone.

8.   Clausewitz, 89.

9.   Clausewitz.

10.   President Bush did not tell the American public to "go shopping" in the wake of the attacks. However, the government did seek to restore public confidence in the economy following the attack. In order to accomplish this feat, the populace needed to return to a sense of normalcy despite the presence of the National Guard at airports, government buildings, and other potential targets. Bush reiterated in speeches on 11 September, 20 September, and 27 September that the military was capable of conducting the mission he directed following the attacks. In a speech to airline workers at O-Hare International Airport in Chicago in 27 September 2001, Bush stated, "Tell the traveling public: Get on board. Do your business around the country. Fly and enjoy America's great destination spots. Get down to Disney World in Florida. Take your families and enjoy life, the way we want it to be enjoyed." George W. Bush in "A Nation Challenged: The President; Bush to Increase Federal Role in Security at Airports," *The New York Times,* 28 September 2001.

11.   Richard Nixon ran as the Republican candidate for president on a platform the promised to restore law and order and ending the draft. The law and order theme appealed to most Americans following protests at the Democratic National Convention in Chicago, the Robert Kennedy and Martin Luther King, Jr. assassinations, and the Tet Offensive. Nixon believed that ending the draft would undermine the protest movement because college-age males would stop protesting once the threat of being drafting ceased to exist. Stephen Ambrose, *Nixon: The Triumph of a Politician 1962-1972*, vol. 2. (New York: Simon and Schuster, 1989), 264–266. Also see Lewis L. Gould, *1968: The Election that Changed America* (Chicago: Ivan R. Dee, 1993).

12.   The 11-15 August 1965 Watts riots in Los Angeles, California is an example of the government's use of policy, in the form of a curfew and martial law, to diminish the populace's passion. The riots started on 11 August after a white police officer attempted to arrest an African-American man for driving intoxicated. The situation gradually escalated after the man resisted arrest. Less than a day later, over 31,000 people were actively rioting in the Watts neighborhood. On 13 August, the acting governor of California, Glenn M. Anderson, mobilized nearly 13,400 National Guardsmen to assist the police after two days of rioting, arson, looting, and violence. In addition, Anderson ordered an immediate curfew and the

authorized the use martial law in South Central Los Angeles. Since the curfew prohibiting the gathering of people in public places, the National Guard units could quickly spot and disperse crowds before they could cause further damage. The combination of the curfew, National Guardsmen, and a cordon around the affected area quickly brought the riots to an end 48 hours later. The National Guard ended operations on 23 August. *Military Support of Law Enforcement during Civil Disturbances: A Report Concerning the California National Guard's Part in Suppressing the Los Angeles Riot, August 1965* (Sacramento: California Office of State Printing, 1966), 9, 38, 58. Also see Gerald Horne, *Fire This Time: The Watts Uprising and the 1960s* (Charlottesville: University Press of Virginia, 1995), 155-163.

13. Clausewitz, 87. Politicians, military officials, and theorists often quote this phase is out of context.

14. Mao wrote *Guerilla Warfare* during the Chinese conflict with Japan in the Second World War. At the time, Mao's forces had not been successful in spreading the communist ideology through much of the country. At the time of writing, his forces were in an alliance with the Nationalist forces to fight the Japanese. Mao Tse-Tung, *Guerrilla Warfare*, trans. Samuel B. Griffith II (Chicago: University of Illinois Press, 2000), 41.

15. Thompson's book contrasts the British experience in Malaya with the early American experience in Vietnam. Since, the book was published in 1966 it failed to include the later American experience in Vietnam. Sir Robert Thompson, *Defeating Communist Insurgency* (St. Petersburg: Hailer Publishing, 1966), 22.

16. Thompson, 142-144. At the tactical level, Clausewitz only concerned himself with the tactical ends and means. Tactics provided the means for an end, namely victory.

17. The Dhofar campaign is explained in detail in Chapter 4.

18. Frank Kitson's *Bunch of Five* attempted to compile lessons from five counterinsurgencies that he fought in following the Second World War. At the end of the book, he offered the reader a list of lessons for future conflicts, which included the idea of integrated campaigns. Other contemporary counterinsurgency theorists agree with this statement. Frank Kitson, *Bunch of Five* (London: Faber and Faber, 1977), 283-284.

19. Galula served as company commander during the French war in Algeria, which he wrote a book about titled *Pacification in Algeria*. His second book attempted to provide a theory of counterinsurgency based on his experiences. Theorist and military professionals in the United States heavily read the book because of Galula's association with the RAND Corporation. However, his scope and depth are somewhat limited due to his rank and position during the conflict. David Galula, *Counterinsurgency Warfare: Theory and Practice* (Westport CT: Praeger Security International, 1964), 46.

20. The Chinese immigrants faced forced resettlement, food restrictions, and other population control measures during the Emergency. However, they were also allowed to form their own Home Guard, conduct local elections, and eventually obtain limited citizenship towards the end of the campaign. The rights the Chinese had during the Emergency depended on their ability to control the local populace and ensure compliance with the Malayan government. In 1955, about 50-percent of the Chinese immigrants living in Malaya were eligible for citizenship because of strict requirements. When the first national government convened in 1955, the Chinese had only 15 seats in the parliament. They also faced significant obstacles in other governmental sectors including the military and police. Karl Hack, "The Malayan Emergency as Counter-Insurgency Paradigm," *Journal of Strategic Studies* 32, no. 3 (June 2009): 383-388, 395.

21. Liberal democracy, also referred to as classical liberalism, is a term that emerged during the Enlightenment in Europe. It applies to governments based on the protection of certain liberties including individual freedoms, equality, separation between the government and religion, open debate (including freedom of the press and assembly), and habit of rational decision making. This study is limited to the does not evaluate population control in authoritarian governments. John Locke's *Letters Concerning Toleration* (1689–92) and *Two Treatises of Government* (1689) and John Stuart Mill's *On Liberty* influenced the tenets of liberal democracy. Paul Berman, *Terror and Liberalism* (New York: W.W. Norton and Company, 2004), xii-xiii.

22. Department of the Army, Field Manual 3-24 *Counterinsurgency* (Chicago: University of Chicago Press, 2007), 180.

23. Department of the Army, Field Manual 1-02 *Operational Terms and Graphics* s.v. "Populace and Resource Control" (Washington, DC: Government Printing Office, 21 September 2004).

24. Clausewitz, 89.

25. Clausewitz, 476.

26. Smith postulated that Clausewitz's theory of war could be reduced to a simple mathematical problem: Capability $=$ Means x Way^2 x 3Will. Means corresponds to the populace according to Clausewitz; therefore, as it is the only variable not manipulated by some mathematical descriptor, it is assigned as the least important variable when assessing a state's capability to conduct war. General Rupert Smith, *The Utility of Force: The Art of War in the Modern World* (New York: Vintage Books, 2007), 244-245.

27. Smith, 245.

28. Mao, 41.

29. Galula, 52.

30. Galula, 81-85.

31. Population-centric counterinsurgency lacks a clear, concise definition within the United States military doctrine. Its emphasis during the surge in Iraq and later in Afghanistan seems to have originated with the interim counterinsurgency manual. Even after the publication of Field Manual 3-24, *Counterinsurgency*, in 2007 it still remained an undefined term. Kilcullen cites German Colonel Reinhard Gehlen to define population-centric counterinsurgency in terms of a struggle with the insurgent for the minds and support of the population. In the end, if the population supports the counterinsurgent, no insurgency should exist. This definition provides a simplistic solution to a complex problem. Commanders on the ground offered Soldiers platitudes stating that the populace was the decisive terrain. Even Galula, who is often championed as one of the primary influences of population-centric counterinsurgency, acknowledged that the problem of the enemy must be addressed first. David Kilcullen, *Counterinsurgency* (Oxford: Oxford University Press, 2010), 6; Galula, 75.

32. Thompson, 50-51.

33. Thompson, 54-57.

34. Kitson, *Bunch of Five*, 282

35. Kitson, 283.

36. Thompson, 146.

37. Mao, 54, 72, 75.

38. David Kilcullen, *The Accidental Guerrilla: Fighting Small Wars in the Midst of a Big One* (Oxford: Oxford University Press, 2009), 267.

39. Kitson included intelligence as one of five aspects for framework operations. He further stated that establishing an effective intelligence organization is a matter of the first importance. Kitson, *Bunch of Five*, 287. Thompson dedicated an entire chapter to the subject. He stated, "No government can hope to defeat a communist insurgent movement unless it gives top priority to building up such an [intelligence] organization." Thompson, 84.

40. Trinquier served in the French Army from the Second World War until the after the coup against de Gaulle in 1961. His experiences with counterinsurgency included experience in both Indochina and Algeria. His book offers lessons learned based primarily on his experiences in Algeria, where he served as an executive officer and regimental commander. He referred to revolutionary warfare as modern. Roger Trinquier, *Modern Warfare: A French View of Counterinsurgency* (Westport CT: Praeger Security International, 1964), 38.

41. Gwynn's collection of ten case studies includes the period from Amritsar City, India in 1919 to Cyprus in 1931. He selected the case studies as representative of the period following the Victorian-era small wars. The book, published in 1936, was written for both military and civil authorities to facilitate understanding between the two entities when the army may be required to fulfill policing duties. Major General Sir Charles W. Gwynn, *Imperial Policing* (London: MacMillan and Co., Ltd., 1936), 1.

42. The term small war had a specific definition at the time Gwynn wrote *Imperial Policing*. A small war in the British lexicon referred to "all campaigns other than those where both the opposing sides consist of regular troops." Small wars included military action against any body that did resemble a western army, including native populations and guerrillas. Small wars typically took place in the developing world. The standard reference was Colonel C. E. Callwell, *Small Wars: Their Principles and Practice*, 3rd ed. (London: HM Stationary Press, 1906), 21. The US Marines published their small wars manual after Gywnn's writing in 1940, and their definition included a more holistic approach. Small wars as defined by the Marines is "an operation undertaken under executive authority, wherein military force is combined with diplomatic pressure in the internal or external affairs of another state whose government is unstable, inadequate, or unsatisfactory for the preservation of life and of such interests as are determined by the foreign policy of our Nation." The subsequent explanation of this definition included a caveat that the other belligerent is not a first-rate power. United States Marine Corps, *Small Wars Manual*, 1940 (Washington, DC: Government Printing Office, 1940), 1-2.

43. Gwynn, 3-4.

44. The British defined two categories of duties in aid of the civil power. The first duty is to provide assistance for the restoration of law and order during disturbances. The second duty is referred to as military assistance, and it was concerned with events like providing basic services following a natural disaster. The primary difference between the two categories is the amount of power the military authority had once aid was requested. Another difference addressed the use of firearms and the rules of engagement, where the second category was much more restrictive in allowing the military authority to use force. This paper is concerned only with the first category of aid. The War Office, *Imperial Policing and Duties in Aid of the Civil Power, 1949* (London: Fosh and Cross Ltd., 1949), 4-5, 17-18, 30-31.

45. Internal security covered the range of military operations that addressed events including assemblies, riots, subversion, insurgency, and rebellion. The 1957 and 1963 versions of this manual included a discussion on the influence of outside actors, specifically communist, and their ability to influence the local populace. The War Office, *Keeping the Peace, Part 1 - Doctrine* (Manchester: HM Stationary Office Press, 1963), 1-2.

46. Ministry of Defence, *Land Operations Volume III – Counter Revolutionary Operations, Part 1 – General Principles* (Manchester: HM Stationary Office Press, 1977), iii.

47. The manual states that policing occurs when three criteria are met that ensure the government protects the rights of the people. First, the enemy is defeated or not capable of challenging the government's sovereignty. Second, the institutions concerning the rule of law are functioning. These include the police, courts, and prisons. Finally, the people must trust the government institutions to resolve disputes. FM 3-24, 246.

48. Angel Rabasa et al., *Money in the Bank: Lessons Learned from Past Counterinsurgency (COIN) Operations* (Arlington, VA: RAND Corporation, 2007), xiv.

49. The 10:1 ratio appears in General Thomas Mataxis's writings on the Reagan Administration's strategy for the Afghan Insurgency. Thomas C. Mataxis, "The Afghan Insurgency and the Reagan Doctrine" in *The History of Guerrilla Warfare* (Ann Arbor: XanEdu, 1994): 7.

50. Some of these studies included historical analysis of the Malayan Emergency and Northern Ireland. James Quinlivan, "Force Requirements in Stability Operations," *Parameters* 25 (Winter 1995-1996): 59-60.

51. Peter J. P. Krause, "Troop Levels in Stability Operations: What We Don't Know," *Center for International Studies* (2007): 1-3.

52. Headquarters, Department of the Army, FMI 3-07.22 *Counterinsurgency Operations* (Washington, DC: Government Printing Office, 2004), 1-13.

53. FM 3-24, 1-13.

54. R. Royce Kneece Jr., *Force Sizing for Stability Operations* (Alexandria: Institute for Defense Analyses, 2010), iii.

55. Kneece, 16.

56. Kneece, 10.

57. Rabasa, xiv.

58. CENTCOM provided this ratio to Krause at the beginning of "the surge." It includes all Iraqi ground force, including the police, not just the forces actually on duty at the time. At any given time, roughly 20-percent of the force is on leave. Krause, 2-3.

59. It should be noted that although Kitson referred to guarding and protection as less skilled functions, he also referred to the operations as the main function of defensive operations. Kitson, 295.

60. Kitson, 296.

61. Trinquier, 41-42.

62. Thompson, 104.

63. Thompson implies that a competing theory at the time insisted that victory was not possible without a ten to one ratio. However, he contrasts the increasing ratio of security forces in Malaya over time to the decreasing ratio of security forces in Vietnam until 1965. Thompson claims that the South Vietnamese government had a force of ratio of 50:1 at the beginning of the war, but by 1965 it had fallen to 10:1. Regardless of the ratio, the South Vietnamese should have had enough forces available to defeat the Viet Cong without the introduction of American troops. Thompson, 48-49.

64. Brian McAllister Linn, *The Philippine War, 1899-1902* (Lawrence: University of Kansas Press, 2000), 125, 209-210.

65. The July 1901 legislation authorized the Insular Constabulary to recruit 162 Soldiers for each province to "make arrests upon reasonable suspicion without warrant for breaches of the peace." Governor Taft also realized the need for native irregular Soldiers to replace the departing Volunteer regiments and authorized the Army to form fifty companies of 104 men, organized along tribal lines, for pacification efforts. Alfred McCoy, *Policing America's Empire* (Madison: University of Wisconsin Press, 2009), 83.

66. McCoy.

67. Linn, 325.

Chapter 3

North-West Frontier

The Guides are an interesting and remarkable Corps. They are formed so that in the same body of men shall be united all the requisites of regular forces troops with the best qualities of guides and spies, thus combining intelligence and sagacity with courage, endurance, and soldierly bearing, and a presence of mind which rarely fails in solitary danger and in trying situations.

- Brigadier A. Roberts to Board on the Administration
19 August 1852

The British experience with the use of local, irregular security forces suggests their importance in assisting the host nation government and counterinsurgent forces. Their successful establishment, training, and employment demonstrate the importance of several prerequisites including partnership with an advisory force, consent of the host nation's government to exist, and that the security force is accountable to the local civil authority. Without these prerequisites, the local, irregular security force could risk illegitimacy in the eyes of the populace, the host nation government, and the counterinsurgent.

In the 1850s, the sun never set on the British Empire. In spite of that fact, British civil authorities had a problem without an apparent solution, the unique characteristics of administering the North-West Frontier (NWF) of British India. The small number of British civil administrators needed a body of men that could enforce the Raj's[1] policy in this volatile region. The British sought to influence the frontier tribes that occupied the mountainous region between the fertile plains of the Punjab and the Kingdom of Afghanistan.[2] The Indian Army[3] lacked the ability to operate efficiently in rugged terrain. As Brigadier Roberts suggested, the British needed a specialized unit with knowledge of the local terrain and tribal dynamics.[4] The military operated in the NWF as an aid to the civil power mission. However, a modern observer would see parallels to many of today's counterinsurgency missions in the same region to include guarding the frontier against criminal elements, escorting civil authorities, and controlling the population. The British raised several local, irregular security forces to control the population, including the Queen Victoria's Own Corps of Guides, the Punjab Irregular Force (PIF)[5], and the Frontier Scouts, to assist the civil authority in the North-West Frontier.

The irregular Soldiers stationed in the NWF executed a number of military operations including small wars,[6] imperial policing,[7] and aid to the civil power.[8] After the First World War the military switched from fighting small wars to control populations and guarding the frontiers to imperial policing.[9] The military assisted the civil administration by escorting government officials, meeting with tribal leaders, providing local security, and when necessary conducting punitive expeditions.[10]

British civil authorities recognized that they needed a local solution in the North-West Frontier because the army lacked British or Indian regiments with the institutional expertise needed in the region.[11] For a variety of reasons the British Army at home and the Indian Army developed into two very different entities. The British Army trained for conventional, European warfare. Conversely, the Indian Army was primarily concerned with enforcement of imperial policy and guerrilla warfare against loosely organized tribal organizations and was referred to as the "sword of the Raj."

The Indian Army's historical ties to the pre-1860 East India Company Army were part of the reason for the differences that developed between the British Army and the Indian Army. The East India Company (EIC) originally established the army and garrisons to protect its commercial interests at the beginning of the 18th-century. Garrisons were spread out along the frontier. As a result of these differences, the Indian Army developed different unit organizations, tactics, and equipment than the British Army at home. Over time, the EIC consolidated its rule and influence in British India. The company divided British possessions into three presidencies, the Bengal, the Madras, and the Bombay, each independent of the others. Each presidency recruited and maintained its own native army. Traditionally, each army developed its own recruiting ground, with preferences for caste, class, and religion of their Soldiers.[12]

The East India Company and its army evolved over the next hundred years until the British government took control following the Indian Mutiny. The EIC consolidated and simplified the relationships between the three presidencies after Parliament passed the Regulating Act of 1773. The following year, the Governor of Bengal, Warren Hastings, took control of the other two presidencies for foreign policy matters.[13] Subsequent acts consolidated the EIC's military affairs. The Commander-in-Chief of the Bengal Army was also the Commander-in-Chief, India. He had general control of the Madras and Bombay armies, but he left the conduct of daily business to the commanders of those armies. In 1858, the Crown took control of India from the EIC following the passage of the Government of India Act. The Governor-General of Bengal's title changed to the Viceroy of India. He represented the Crown in India, but remained subject to British cabinet and parliamentary oversight. He also had a personal military advisor with the title, Military Secretary.[14]

In 1754, the British government started to supplement the East India Company Army with regiments from the British Army.[15] When these regiments were assigned to India, they were referred to the Army in India. The government could assign British home regiments to India for long tours of duty, up to sixteen years. Each presidency's army had British Army units assigned to it, although the relationship between the two armies was not always congenial. These regiments took orders from the military authority in India, not the War Office in London.[16]

Regiments in India often had different priorities and operational methods than British regiments serving at home or in other imperial possessions that resulted in a schism between the home army and the Indian army. These differences could and did taint officers' careers. British officers, especially from the upper class, often viewed service in India or in the Indian Army as beneath them. Many of them elected to go on half-pay while their regiment served in India or tried to purchase commissions in other British regiments. This problem diminished after Queen Victoria issued a Royal Warrant banning the purchasing and selling of commissions, as well as the half-pay system, in 1871.[17]

However, service in the Indian Army offered a number of advantages for aspiring junior officers that lacked clear paths to wealth and fame. First, both civil administrators and military leaders encouraged individual initiative, flexibility, resourcefulness, and physical fitness even at the subaltern level.[18] Next, the average junior officer in the Indian Army earned nearly 60-percent more than his British Army counterpart due to a combination of higher pay and a lower cost of living. Officers enjoyed a semi-aristocratic status that they could not otherwise afford in England. Finally, the rate of promotion in the Indian Army outpaced their counterparts at home, especially post-1860.[19]

Few of the British regiments served in the North-West Frontier. In fact, few Indian Army regiments served in the frontier. Instead, the British used a combination of locally administered militias and regiments to guard the border. In order to understand why Lawrence brothers sought to create the Punjab Irregular Force and the Frontier Scouts, it is necessary to understand how British policy regarding the North-West Frontier and its relationship to the Punjab.

Figure 3. Map of the Bengal, Bombay, and Madras Presidencies in 1893.

Source: J. G. Bartholomew, ed., *Constable's Hand Atlas of India* (London: Archibald Constable and Sons, 1893), Plate 16. CGSC Copyright Registration #12-1354 C/E

The Indian Army and the Punjab

The history of British involvement in the NWF is linked to British involvement in the Punjab. The British fought two wars against the Sikhs in the Punjab. The First Sikh War, December 1845-March 1846, resulted in the Treaty of Lahore. The Sikhs ceded a significant portion of its land to the British. However, the British allowed the Maharaja, an infant, to retain the crown if the Sikhs accepted British oversight. Sir Henry Lawrence assumed the role of the British Resident, but he left the job less than two years to return to England to recuperate from illness. Finally, the Sikhs accepted limitations on the size and composition of the army. The Second Sikh War started on 18 April 1848 when a British political officer and his military escort were murdered in Multan. Parts of the Sikh army rebelled throughout the Punjab against their British advisors. The resulting military expedition defeated the Sikh army and Afghan reinforcements.[20]

The British annexed the Punjab on 29 March 1849 following the Second Sikh War and maintained control until independence in 1947.[21]

The Board of Administration, specifically Sir John Lawrence,[22] viewed the Sikhs as a threat since some of the Sikh regiments had mutinied against the British during the Second Sikh War. Lawrence had the Punjabi regiments disarmed and then demobilized. The British initially thought that disarming the Sikhs in the Punjab would prevent another Sikh uprising in the future. However, this policy presented an enormous security problem for the new Board of Administration. First, it created 50,000-60,000 unemployed Sikhs, all former Soldiers.[23] Second, it exposed the Punjab to raids by the frontier tribes, because the Bengal Army lacked the manpower or skills necessary to protect the Punjab.[24]

The first problem was significant because the Europeans trained the Sikh army prior to the two wars with the British. The Sikhs were ripe for military recruitment. The Bengal Army took control of some of the regiments that remained loyal during the wars. Lord Dalhousie also allowed the other presidency armies to recruit a small percentage of Sikhs into their regiments not to exceed more than 25-percent of the unit. This policy moved some of the unemployed Sikhs outside of the Punjab. Additionally, they had to be recruited from regiments that remained loyal to the British during the Second Sikh War that the Bengal Army had not accepted. However, several military commanders considered the Sikhs unreliable given the Sikhs' strong sense of nationalism.[25] The feeling would change after the Indian Mutiny, and by the late 1860s the Punjab was the largest recruiting ground for the Indian Army.[26]

The second problem, the small size of the Bengal Army, was a source of concern for the British political officers. They assessed two threats on the frontier, the Kingdom of Afghanistan and the frontier tribes. Afghanistan and the British had already fought one war, the First Afghan War, 1839-1842, and Afghanistan had provided the Sikhs with troops during the Second Sikh War. In some cases, Afghanistan's influence on the frontier tribes contributed to the security problem.[27] The British were primarily concerned with control of the Punjabi plains because its economic and agricultural value. They left control of the mostly barren frontier to the tribes.[28] This policy left a tribal zone three hundred miles long by one hundred miles wide in between the Punjab and the Kingdom of Afghanistan that both administrations sought to influence.[29] Several tribes lived in both the tribal area and the British area. Even after the demarcation of the Durand Line in 1894 following an agreement with the Kingdom of Afghanistan, the tribes did not recognize the line as a formal border. Furthermore, the British lacked the manpower to enforce it.[30] In fact, the British did not restrict movement across the frontier and even allowed tribesmen to carry weapons until they crossed the Indus River.[31] An estimated 100,000 men of fighting age lived on the frontier.[32]

The size of the frontier tribes, the tribal dynamics, and the lack of available manpower influenced how the British administered the NWF. Sir John Lawrence argued that an entire division of Soldiers could not secure the frontier.[33] As a result, the British sought to limit their contact with the tribes after annexation of the Punjab. The British administered the North-West Frontier separately from the rest of British India based upon indirect rule. The Lieutenant Governor of the Punjab controlled frontier policy from Peshawar.[34] He in turn worked with a deputy commissioner in each of the six districts. The amount of contact that the political agents had with the tribe varied on the guidance given to them by the Governor of the Punjab and the Board of Administration.[35]

The British used a variety of policies from the 1850s until independence in 1947 to maintain their influence with the frontier tribes and the Kingdom of Afghanistan.[36] The civil administration referred to the these methods as the "close border policy," "forward policy," and the "modified forward policy" Each system relied on the British's ability to co-opt or bribe the tribes for good behavior and withhold incentives when the tribes defied British wishes. One major difference between the closed border policy and two forward policies was the location of military.

Advocates of "closed border policy", including Sir John Lawrence, wanted no interference with Afghanistan and as little contact with the frontier tribes as possible. This policy sought "non-aggression on tribal territory and non-interference in tribal affairs."[37] The tribes could cross into British land, but the district officers would not cross into the tribal lands. The British paid the tribes subsidies to remain peaceful, and they would levy fines against the tribes when they broke the agreement. The tribes quickly figured out the inherent flaw of this system, which required the British to adopt harsher methods. When a hostile tribe crossed the border and committed a crime, a punitive expedition reasserted British power as a method of deterrence. Unfortunately, this policy meant that most of the civilians only saw the British when they conducted a punitive raid.[38]

In 1876, the "forward policy" sought to extend the Raj's control as close to the border of Afghanistan as possible, and if necessary beyond it for punitive operations against hostile tribes. The British government was concerned with possible future aggression by the Kingdom of Afghanistan and Imperial Russia. The British civil government could introduce law and administration into the tribal areas to pacify the frontier tribes. The forward policies sought to push the troops forward into the tribal areas as part of a comprehensive system of maintaining influence with the frontier tribes.[39] The military also took over the defense of strategic places along the frontier, most notably the Khyber Pass, to ensure that they did not need to fight the tribes for them in event of another war with Afghanistan.[40]

Under both the closed border policy and the forward policy, the military conducted punitive expeditions to reassert British control over a certain tribe or area. The British conducted punitive expeditions in response to various offenses made by the tribes against British interests. The offenses included crimes such as murder of British administers, raids against frontier posts, theft of British material, and several lesser offenses. Field Marshal Lord Roberts[41] described a typical punitive expedition in his memoir. A British column of no more than 1,500 Soldiers moved into the tribal land. Since the British rarely caught the tribesmen directly responsible for the crime, they usually identified a village, razed it, fined the remaining tribesmen, and retired to their frontier garrisons. Other tribes usually observed the expedition, and the British hoped that the display of resolve sufficiently dissuaded other tribes from committing offenses against British interests.[42] Examples of punitive expeditions conducted during the enforcement of the forward policy include the Waziristan operation in 1894-1895, the Chitral relief campaign of 1895, and the Tirah expedition of 1897-1895.[43]

The British political officers modified the forward policy to take advantage of Baluchistan's unique culture. Unlike the Pashtun tribes, the Baluchs have a hierarchical tribal structure, allowing the British to co-opt the tribes through the leaders (tumandars). The Sandeman System allowed the army to occupy certain key points, linking them together with roads to allow the army to reinforce other garrisons quickly, and adopting a hands-off approach to the tribes as long as they remained peaceful. Sandeman paid the tribes subsidies to remain peaceful, provide information, and to perform other civil tasks. The British effectively ruled Baluchistan only through use of the forward policy.[44]

The final method is referred to as the "modified forward policy." This policy sought to extend the Sandeman system into Waziristan following the 1919-1920 war. The British concentrated troops at key locations, paid local tribesman, called *khassadars*, to report information and supplement the regular forces. However, the policy was not successful, since the Wazirs resisted all attempts at pacification.[45]

The nature of warfare in the NWF differed greatly from the rest of the Empire under every one of the border policies. The unique terrain, the tribal dynamics, and the lack of intelligence created conditions that differed from western civilized warfare. The frontier extended for 704-miles and lacked an internationally accepted and demarcated border. In the NWF, the civil administration dispersed individual units over large tracts of land. The open, rocky terrain did not favor large-scale military operations. It is a chain of mountains, largely devoid of vegetation, bisected by four passes. These four passes were the primary invasion routes into and out of British India. Deep river valleys further complicate travel in this region.[46] The broken, mountainous terrain prevented the British from using massed, close-order formations that dominated the European battlefield. It also prevented the British from using their cavalry in its traditional exploitation role.

No drill book existed for the training that the irregular regiments needed to secure the frontier. These forces spent a majority of their time guarding the frontier from raiders. Regiments could rarely concentrate for training, which meant the British and native junior officers and their NCOs were responsible for ensuring their men were constantly ready for war. The training was a combination of experience gathered from previous conflicts and the projection of how officers believed war would change with the introduction of new weapons.[47]

The frontier tribes consisted of several different Pushtun and Pukhtun[48] tribes, which together the British referred to as Pathans, and adhered to a system of unwritten laws known as the *Pushtunwali*. The *Pushtunwali* code governed individual and collective relations between the Pathans. Although the exact number of *Pushtunwali* principles varies from tribes to tribe, some of the principles were close to be universally accepted. *Badal*, a blood feud, is the first principle. *Badal* refers the idea of that a tribesman must exact vengeance for a wrong done to his family. If he dies before completing the act, then a relative must complete the duty. The principle of *badal* is similar to the Old Testament concept of an eye for an eye.[49] The British believed that most of these conflicts originated from issues with women, gold, and land.[50] The second principle, *nanawati*, refers to right of asylum. The Pathans accepted that any man could request asylum in the presence of the Koran and that he could not deny the request. The third principle is *melmastia*, or hospitality. The final principle is the duty to protect *hamsayas*, people who assist the tribesmen with the daily functioning of the tribes. *Hamsayas* do not have to be Pushtun. The British political officers often took advantage of this aspect of the code to travel in the tribal areas.[51] With the exception of one tribal area, the tribes lacked a formal organization to enforce the code.[52] In theory, failure to adhere to the code resulted in shame on the individual, his family, and his tribe.[53]

Figure 4. North-West Frontier.
Source: Author created.

The tribes did not have formal military units. A tribal assembly, or *jirga*,[54] decided to form a *lashkar*,[55] elected leaders, and decided tribal levies, and determined the campaigns goals.[56] The tribal commanders were generally a charismatic male or religious leader. However, command of a *lashkar* was not similar to command of a British Indian unit. Tribesmen, or *lashkarwali*, provided their own campaigning equipment, arms, and mount. Each tribesman determined his own contribution to the campaign. He determined the amount of risk that he would take in battle, and he decided if wanted to return home when his food ran out.[57] The *lashkarwali* rarely massed into a formation that stood and fought against an advancing column.

The tribes had significant advantages over British regiments due to the nature of hill warfare. The British formations had a hard time identifying objectives that produced decisive results against a tribe. Even with the use of the native troops, punitive expeditions operated with minimal information. Tribes took sanctuary in Afghanistan or with neighboring tribes when punitive expeditions approached their villages.

Since the British expeditions traveled forward into enemy territory, the enemy had the advantage of knowledge of the terrain and the ability to observe British troops advancing with their trains. As a result, the tribesmen could pick the time and location to attack the invaders.[58] Finally, the *lashkars* could move greater distances without the burden of a logistical column. Sir Richard Temple explained in 1855, "the enemy does not possess troops that stand to be attacked, not defensible posts to be taken, nor innocent subjects to be spared. He has only rough hills to be penetrated, robber fastnesses to be scaled, and dwellings containing people, all of them to a man concerned in hostilities."[59]

Queen Victoria's Own Corps of Guides

Temple's comments summarized some of the unique conditions of the NWF that the civil authorities and the military had to contend with in order to enact British policy. The regular army was not suited for the task. Regular troops considered service in the austere conditions of the frontier unpopular at best, and as punishment at worst. During the First Afghan War, Sir Henry Lawrence noticed that British and Indian forces had significant difficulties negotiating the frontier terrain and working with the tribes.[60] The regular regiments had too much baggage when campaigning, rendering them ineffective against the hit-and-run tactics of the frontier tribes.[61] Additionally, Soldiers from the traditional recruiting grounds of the Presidency armies did not have knowledge of the frontier tribes, nor the skills required for mountain warfare.

Lawrence resolved to create a force of local guides and interpreters to address this problem in the future conflicts. Lawrence required the Guides to conduct three missions, act as guides in the field, gather intelligence within and outside the Punjab, and to train to conduct offensive operations.[62] He obtained permission from Lord Dalhousie, the Governor-General of India, to raise a corps of guides, one company of infantry and one cavalry troop in December 1846.[63] Colonel G. J. Younghusband recorded some additional information about Lawrence's order to raise the Guides in his history. He stated that Lawrence needed a mobile unit of troops to help administer the Punjab following the First Sikh War. The British had very few troops stationed in the Punjab at the time, and most of those were located at Lahore. The new formation of troops needed to be highly mobile and skilled in gathering intelligence.

In addition to being granted permission to raise the Corps of Guides, the Governor-General gave Lawrence permission to select one British lieutenant to command the force.[64] Lawrence specified that the officer's duties included the ability to direct their operations, record the information gather, instruct the guides on their duties in support of the army. The officer also served a liaison between the unit and Lawrence.[65] He selected Lieutenant Harry Lumsden.[66] He possessed qualities that Lawrence thought were necessary for the irregular formation, including a natural ability for war, communicated well with the natives, and he had a calm demeanor even in an emergency. He was the veteran of a number of other campaigns.[67]

Service for a British officer in the irregular units offered challenging work. The officers were chronically understaffed compared to their fellow officers in the regular army. The allotment of officers in an irregular unit was usually one-sixth the allotment of a regular native unit.[68] The units guarding the frontier were constantly on alert for raiders. The pace of operations could be punishing. Officers had to balance guarding the frontier, escorting civil servants and other British subjects, and constantly training their Soldiers for combat in support of a punitive expedition. The British conducted 52 punitive operations and several smaller raids into the tribal areas between 1849-1914.[69] In addition to their military duties, several officers also doubled as civil servants on the frontier, paying subsidies and levying fines as part of the British policy to maintain influence with the tribes.[70]

First, Lumsden needed to determine the type of the men he wanted for the local security force. Unlike most units in 1846, Lumsden did not base the recruitment of the first two guide companies on the "class" system prevalent in the Presidency armies. Up to that point, the British considered a person's class to be an extremely important tool for recruiting, as it was a predictor of his suitability for military life.[71] The British defined class a combination of the race, religion, and caste of a tribesman.[72] Not all classes were allowed to carry arms. The British recruited the following tribes from within India: Rajput, Hindustani and Punjabi Brahman, Punjabi Mussalman, Hindustani Mussalman, Jats, Gujars, Pathans, and Moguls. The British also recruited Soldiers from outside of India, predominately the trans-frontier Pathans and the Gurkhas.[73] Tribes were then subdivided by religion, and then by country. Adding to the complexity of the class system, the Muhammadans were a mixed tribe, primarily Rajput, which had converted to Islam.[74] The Sikhs are a religious sect with members in every tribe, although most came from the Jats.[75] Finally, the British referred to some tribes by the geographical region where they lived, such as the Dogras.[76] As a result of this complex system, the British identified and tracked the inclusion of 29 classes in the Indian Army in 1904.[77]

In contrast to the traditional recruiting practices, Lumsden took a personal interest in obtaining the Soldiers he wanted for the Guides. There was no shortage of men that interviewed for a job in the corps.[78] Several contemporary historians and social scientists have tried to explain why the British were able to recruit thousands of natives for service in the Indian Army, but most agree that natives simply sought a better life in the army.[79] Lumsden interviewed each man with an interest to his background prior to enrolling him into the regiment. He recruited strictly from the higher castes.[80] As a result, the companies were so mixed that the language spoken in camp was an assortment of different local dialects.[81] Lumsden offered them a job with regular pay, above and beyond the normal native stipend, and the stability that life as a raider lacked.[82] Additionally, it seems that Lumsden sought out a fringe criminal element that was used to living in the mountains. Lumsden recruited the remainder of his force from local chiefs' families.[83]

Recruiting from the local population benefitted the British military and the civil authorities with the administration of the Punjab. In addition to gaining knowledge of the frontier, it had the potential to reduce violence. Service in the Guides tied prominent tribes to the unit's officers and sometimes the district officers, since elders were required to vouch for the character of their recruits. The story of Dilawur Khan's also illustrates another aspect of this benefit. He was an example of a tribesman originally destined for priesthood, but found kidnapping bankers in the frontier more lucrative. Despite his background, Lumsden recruited him service in the Guides, where he excelled as native leader. Dilawur's story illustrated another important aspect of controlling the frontier with locally raised forces: Every raider employed by the British prevented that tribesman from committing crimes and undermining British rule.[84]

The Guides participated in several military operations prior to and during the Second Sikh War. During their first action in July 1847, Lumsden led a group of twenty guides and a troop of Sikh cavalry into the village of Mugh Darah to capture a noted raider who had kidnapped a number of Hindu businessmen. When Lumsden led his men into the village at first light, he discovered that the Sikh cavalry had refused to follow him into a narrow defile. However, every one of the guides had made the trip, surrounded the village, and disarmed the surprised criminals.[85] Lumsden's force had disarmed and captured a force with less than a third of the troops that were deemed necessary for the mission. The Guides performed these civil support missions until the outbreak of the Second Sikh War, receiving the commendations from both commanders and civil servants.[86] During the Second Sikh War the Guides remained loyal to the British and fought at the Battles of Chillianwallah and Rawalpindi, conducted the initial boat crossing of Indus River to allow the capture of Peshawar, and chased Afghans attempting to reinforce the rebels back to the Khyber Pass.[87] Although Lts. Lumsden and Hodson were mentioned in the dispatches, Lumsden felt that the Guides did not receive the praise that they deserved for their service.[88]

The Punjab Irregular Force

Following on the success of the Corps of Guides during the Second Sikh War, Sir Henry Lawrence sought permission from Lord Dalhousie to raise an irregular force to replace the unreliable police levies that guarded the frontier.[89] On 18 May 1849, Lord Dalhousie ordered Lawrence to raise an irregular force, the Punjab Irregular Force (PIF), consisting of ten regiments, five infantry and five cavalry.[90] The PIF also incorporated four Sikh battalions previously formed to guard the frontier, the Scinde Camel Corps, and the Corps of Guides.[91]

Lawrence's request to form an irregular force to guard the frontier was not a new idea. In 1846, the Sind Force, consisting of the Scinde Irregular Horse, formed with the purpose of guarding the Sind frontier from frontier Baluchi tribes that also raided across the border. Initially, the PIF resembled the Sind Force in structure, numbers, and equipment.[92] However, the similarities stopped with the organization and equipment of the units.

Since its inception, the PIF generated controversy over who controlled the unit. Lawrence wanted a force answerable to the local administration, but Lord Napier, Command-in-Chief, India, wanted control of the unit. In October 1850, Lord Dalhousie decided that to break with the model of the Sind Force. Instead of reporting the Bengal Army command, the PIF answered to the local authority, the Board of Administration, in order to "render it expedient to secure the on the distant frontier."[93] The Governor of the Punjab reported on the PIF to the Foreign Office.[94] Sir Charles Napier, the Commander-in-Chief, India complained to Lord Dalhousie that he although controlled all of the regular Soldiers in the army; he could not move a single sentry in the PIF.[95]

Lord Dalhousie limited the PIF's deployment to the Punjab and the NWF.[96] In effect, he acknowledged the unique nature of warfare in the Punjab and the frontier by making the PIF a local force, answerable to the district officials, that could quickly respond to raids, civil emergencies, etc., without the bureaucracy of a regular military command.[97] It took advantage of the fact that the Indian officers and NCOs had intimate knowledge of the local terrain, customs, and language. The limitation also enhanced the PIF's ability to conduct civil tasks including paying subsidies to peaceful tribes, safeguarding livestock and property, escorting British officials and citizens, and collecting tolls and taxes.

In addition to its civil tasks, the PIF also assumed responsibility for guarding the border between Kohat and Mithunkote.[98] The PIF's initial employment along the frontier demonstrated the difficulty of the task that they were assigned. The 12,800 Soldiers of the PIF took responsibility for a defensive system that included 15 forts and about 50 outposts that guarded key locations along the NWF border. The PIF never had the manpower to properly secure the border and prevent all of the raiders' penetrations. If raiders attacked an outpost there was little chance of reinforcement. The Bengal Army in Peshawar supported the PIF with nearly 10,820 regular British and Indian troops, but its primary job was to repulse any foreign invasion by Afghanistan or Russia.[99] The regular regiments could provide troops to reinforce the PIF in the event of a large tribal penetration of the frontier border.[100]

The PIF never had enough Soldiers to conduct both missions simultaneously without assuming some risk. In late 1851, raiders attacked a detachment of thirty Guides sent to guard a survey party in the Peshawar Valley. Although the Guides repelled the attack, they lost a number of Soldiers in the attack.[101] When the tribes organized their efforts, they could overrun the PIF's small outposts and defensive positions. The 5th Punjab Infantry, a 900-Soldier PIF unit, provided an example of how overextended the PIF was on the frontier. In March 1852, the unit guarded a 200-mile section of the frontier by manning a series of 16 outposts and number of smaller positions.[102] Even when the unit was at full strength, the 5th Punjab Infantry had no more than 4.5 Soldiers to guard each mile against tribal incursions. At best, the Soldiers in the PIF hoped to inflict as much damage as they received by quickly reinforcing isolated outposts and conducting punitive raids.

In November 1846, Sir Henry Lawrence received permission to raise the Frontier Brigade to conduct the civil and military missions on the frontier. Originally, the Frontier Brigade consisted of four regiments of local Sikh infantry.[103] Each regiment received four British officers appointed from the other regular British Indian armies.[104] The officers were selected based on their service reputation, not seniority or patronage. They were primarily veterans from other imperial conflicts including the First Afghan War.[105] Generally, officers selected for the PIF also appreciated the break from the minutiae of garrison life that work on the frontier offered.[106] The Indian officers were recruited from the sons of tribal chiefs.[107] Together the British and Indian officers formed a symbiotic relationship. The British officers had knowledge of the tactics and employment of the technology developed during previous imperial wars, while the Indian officers had knowledge of the local tribal structure and terrain. Finally, Lord Dalhousie granted the Board of Administration permission to recruit a small amount of Punjabi, including the recently demobilized Sikhs, to serve as Soldiers. Given the sheer amount of unemployed Soldiers in the Punjab that wanted to return to an honorable profession, the Sikhs picked for the PIF tended to be the best of the former Sikh Army.[108]

Officers were expected to learn how to counter the raiders' tactics on the job using a unique set of small-unit tactics that emphasized offensive action and security. Due to the broken terrain, officers drilled marksmanship, physical fitness, discipline, and skirmishing tactics to counter the enemy's tactics.[109] Drill provided the basis for discipline and effective training in the irregular regiments. In 1855, General Sir Samuel Browne, a future commander of the PIF, recommended that new officers should immediately learn drill, so that they could in turn teach the NCOs and Soldiers.[110] Drill provided the basis for mountain warfare tactics. Thus, the drill practiced by the regiments was not parade field drill. To illustrate this point, three of the basic drills that every irregular regiment practiced were the taking a piquet, defending a piquet, and moving out of a piquet. The last drill was described as one of the hardest to execute under fire.[111] Captain, J. L. Vaughan, Commander of the 5th Punjab Infantry, one of the original PIF units, used to conduct the drills force-on-force to reinforce rivalry between units. Both British and native officers could have the unit execute the drill again if they made mistakes.[112] As a result of this training regimen, the regiment quickly gained expertise in mountain warfare tactics.

The British and native officers developed a symbiotic relationship when it came to training the irregular troops. Commanders, especially new ones, often sought advice from the native officers.[113] The relationship between the British officers and the native Soldiers reflected an almost paternalistic style, however, the British officers still had to earn their respect. The British appreciated the native sense of humor, knowledge, and in return the native Soldiers maintained an unquestionable loyalty to their officers.[114] Discipline was rarely a problem with the native troops even through the Articles of War for Native Troops did not apply to the PIF.[115] Vaughan praised the native officers' ability to control the Soldiers. He commented that native officers commanded their charges equally well in garrison and the field.[116] Furthermore, the trust and competence built during training allowed officers to give native officers and NCOs command of some of the smaller frontier outposts.[117]

The officers, both British and native, were expected to display initiative and to make recommendations concerning changes to the PIF's tactics and equipment. The commanders quickly determined that the standard issued uniform and kit was not suitable for irregular work. The enemy wore clothes that allowed them to move quickly and to blend in with the terrain.[118] The regular regiments retained the scarlet tunic of the British Army; however, the scarlet uniform proved impractical for scouting and piquet duty on the frontier. Lumsden adopted khaki uniforms for the Guides in 1846, and the PIF followed suit in 1851.[119] Following the 1863-1864 Umbeylah campaign and Black Mountain campaign in 1868, the commanding general, Sir Neville Chamberlain, recommended further adjustments to the PIF's equipment and baggage. He wanted them reduced to make the PIF more mobile enabling it to keep pace with the enemy.[120]

Two other organizational initiatives ensured that the irregular units learned from each other's experience. The PIF was usually on alert for raiders when it was not actively campaigning in the frontier. As a result, the force was typically spread out along a series of forts and outposts that made concentrating the regiments for training difficult. Additionally, since the PIF was not part of the regular army, it did not have an obligation to produce reports to communicate lessons learned while conducting operations. Additionally, the command was not responsible for developing a doctrine for hill warfare.[121] Brigadier Chamberlain introduced the first initiative, the annual encampment of the force for practicing tactics starting in 1862.[122] Vaughan felt these exercises produced good results in battle.[123]

The second initiative was the publication of a PIF journal that passed lessons onto the next generation of officers. In 1865, the Force published a manual of standing orders for the regiments. Furthermore, the command developed a series of circulars to standardize training on the frontier.[124]

These initiatives designed to share knowledge and practice frontier tactics allowed the PIF to remain successful during punitive operations. They allowed the PIF to remain proficient with the current practices despite the fact that PIF spent most of their time guarding the border, especially when compared to the regular army. Captain W. James, the Commissioner of Peshawar, observed that the while the PIF was driving the enemy up one hill, the regular army was retreating under the same pressure on the neighboring hill.[125] The PIF was so successful during the period up to and including the Mutiny, that the rest of the native regiments in the British Indian Army were remodeled to resemble its organization.[126] Chamberlain felt that the PIF had gotten so proficient at punitive operations that he wanted units to emphasize the civilian duties of the "watch and ward" mission.[127]

Although the PIF spent most of its time guarding the frontier until the 1890s, it also conducted operations with the regular army regiments. The Guides and the PIF often served as both scouts and piquets for the main body of a punitive expedition. In this role, they gathered intelligence, protected the regular army, and guarded any retreats. When the main body halted for long periods of time, the irregular forces often manned sangars.[128] The PIF conducted 51 expeditions with and without regular army regiments between 1849-1908. During the 1852 Waziris, 1853 Shiranis, 1857 Bozdars, and 1880 Black Mountain campaigns, the PIF provided all of the troops involved in the punitive expedition.[129] No commander criticized the PIF for their ability to work with regular troops. In fact, in most expeditions it seemed that the PIF conducted their job and some additional duties.[130]

The Indian Mutiny of 1857 had a lasting legacy on the PIF proportional to its extraordinary feats during the conflict. The unit displayed their resilience and their ability to perform civil and military missions. The Indian Mutiny occurred for a variety of reasons, but it resulted in many of the native regiments in the Bengal Army murdering their officers due to ethnic or religious loyalties.[131] In the Punjab, Sir James Lawrence sought to prevent the spread of the mutiny to any of the Bengal regiments. He quietly disbanded four questionable Bengal regiments in the shadow of four loaded artillery pieces before they had the chance to rebel.[132] However, not all of the regiments were suspect. The various battalions and regiments of the PIF remained loyal to a man. All of the native officers and NCOs of the 1st Sikh Infantry signed a petition asking to be sent against the mutineers.[133] The PIF received orders to secure key locations within the Punjab, disarm native regiments, and secure the frontier from possible Afghan interference. Other regiments, including the 1st Punjab Infantry, the 4th Sikhs, and the Guides, marched to Delhi as part a relief column.

The march to Delhi is one of the Guides' most impressive feats in support of the regular army. The Guides were notified of the Mutiny and their mission on 13 May 1857. The regiment marched from Mardan to Delhi, a distance of 580 miles, in only 26 days despite the summer heat.[134] The Guides entered the battle only thirty minutes after arriving in Delhi. During the siege of Delhi, the regiment repulsed 26 attacks against the right flank of the British Army.[135] Field Marshal Roberts singled out the Guides and 1st Punjab Infantry, PIF, in his memoir dealing with the battle.[136]

Following the Indian Mutiny, the British government struggled with how to secure India, especially the frontier, if some of the native troops could not trusted.[137] In July 1858, Major General Jonathan Peel, Secretary of State for War, chaired a government committee to consider the question.[138] The committee agreed that Great Britain lacked the manpower and finances to secure India using the British Army. During the Mutiny, only 23,000 British Soldiers were available to participate in the campaign.[139] The fact that local, irregular Soldiers cost less than regular Soldiers of the British army to train, equip, and maintain was one solution. A British regiment cost more than double an Indian regiment to maintain.[140] The Commission also considered using mercenary troops from other countries with similar climates. However, Sir John Lawrence opposed the idea on basis that every mercenary used in India ensured a native warrior was unemployed. He suggested that these displaced Soldiers would be a source of trouble in any future government.[141]

The Peel Commission reaffirmed Lumsden's recruitment strategy.[142] In their report, the commission recommended that the future army recruit from a wide variety of classes to prevent a monopoly on military service by one class. Additionally, individual units should mix recruitment in terms of caste and religion.[143] The commission used the "divide and rule" policy to make the three Presidency Armies separate and distinct with the idea that they could generate rivalry between the various units. In the PIF, British exploited the religious differences between the Sikhs and Muslims. This policy created "class companies" where each company was comprised entirely of one class.[144] No one class could exceed more than half of the regiment's authorized strength.[145]

The PIF earned a reputation as one of the best units in the Indian Army because of it service during the Mutiny and the subsequent punitive expeditions. However, the military chain of command finally won the battle to control the PIF in 1886. The PIF ceased to be an irregular security force, and it transitioned into a regular unit. It amalgamated with the Bengal Army, although the army did not fully achieve full integration of the PIF until implementation of Kitchener's reforms in 1903.[146] The most important impact of this transformation in the Punjab was the fact that the Punjab Frontier Force ceased to report to the civil authority. Instead, it now took orders from the commander of the Indian Army.[147] In the end, the PIF would still spend most of its time on the frontier, and it remained an "elite" unit in the Indian Army, due its ability to fight in the hostile terrain. All of the regiments added the initials "FF" to their titles – Frontier Force as a source of pride and inspiration.[148]

The Frontier Scouts

With the loss of the PIF to the regular army, the government needed a new unit that could fulfill the PIF's original obligations to provide local security along the border of the province. Simultaneous to Kitchener's reforms of the Indian Army, Lord Curzon, the new Viceroy of India, implemented a series of reforms related to the frontier that created the North-West Frontier Province (NWFP) in 1900. It separated the administration of the frontier from the government of the Punjab. The NWFP now had the same provincial institutions as the rest of British India.[149] The Indian Penal Code now applied in the NWFP and there were functional judicial systems to implement it.[150] In addition to the army, the Frontier Constabulary and some local militias provided policing and border control in the province.[151] Lord Curzon's solution to the security problem was to put all of the existing frontier militias under one command, the Frontier Corps.

The Frontier Corps started as a series of local militias in the late 1870s and 1880s. The militias included the Khyber Rifles, the North and South Waziristan Militias, and the Tochi Scouts. The early militias barely resembled a military formation. The men did not drill. They did not shave or wear uniforms. In fact, the Khyber Rifles originally wore only a small red patch on the back of their *pagri* to identify them as a militiaman.[152] The Frontier Scouts escorted the political officers into the tribal lands under the forward policy.

The frontier militias served a in a variety of roles, primarily in their locality but also in times of war. Most of the units served in specialized roles that assisted the political agent's local agenda. The British formed the Khyber Rifles after the Second Afghan War because Chamberlain's invasion column was stalled at the pass by the tribes.[153] The formation of a militia answerable to the British, and paid for by the British, could alleviate this problem of free passage through the pass should there be another war with Afghanistan. In another instance, the British raised the Chitral Scouts in 1900 specifically to scout for Russian invaders near the Baroghil and Dorah passes.[154] These units could police the frontier, especially Waziristan.[155] The militias provided intelligence and an early warning for the regular regiments. They also provided the first line of defense for their villages. Although the Frontier Scouts were not obligated to serve outside of their locality such as the Guides and the PIF, certain units occasionally volunteered to service on punitive expeditions. As an example, the Khyber Rifles participated in the Black Mountain expedition in 1888 and again in 1891.[156]

Lord Curzon insisted on seconded British officers from the army to serve as the officer corps in the Frontier Corps to provide training and leadership.[157] Prior to the seconding of British military officers, most of the militias had a political officer assigned to them. However, the political officer did not always have the extensive military background necessary to handle the daily tasks of commanding and training a militia. The assignment of military officers helped professionalize the militias, but the militia also reflected the quality of trainer.

During World War I, the quality of British officer assigned to the militia decreased as the war progressed due to the demands of the regular army. British officers did not seek appointments in the Frontier Corps, but instead sought employment with the British and Indian Army in Europe, Palestine, and Mesopotamia.[158] Only after a number of skirmishes in Gomal resulted in heavy casualties, did the military try to rectify the problem. The military created a number of schools to train officers and NCOs assigned to the Frontier Corps on mountain warfare.[159]

After the First World War, the British authorities suffered a series of defeats in campaigns, namely the Third Afghan War and the 1919 Waziristan campaign that relied heavily on the Frontier Corps. The militias lacked the number of Soldiers and officers necessary to truly pacify the frontier. This problem existed with the PIF, but since the militias did not have to serve outside their home area, reinforcements could be days away. At the start of the Waziristan campaign, Cummings' detachment had to put their Wazir Soldiers in jail, destroyed their arms and outpost, and retreated during the Battle of Palosina and Ahnai in December 1919 because they lacked the number of Soldiers to guard the outpost during the uprising.[160]

Officers did not only have to fear the threat of violence from raiders. Sometimes, their own men could kill them in the middle of the night. The Third Afghan War resulted in native Soldiers murdering their officers out of tribal or religious loyalties. The Khyber Rifles were disbanded on 17 May 1919 during the Third Afghan War because the British commanders felt they might rebel.[161] However, the majority of the Frontier Scouts remained loyal during tribal uprising. One documented case in the South Waziristan Militia is the murder of Captain J.B. Bowring by Sepoy Kabul Khan. Bowring had slept with feet towards Mecca and offended Kabul. The British officers knew that they needed to thread a fine line between military justice and the risk of inciting a rebellion inside the small outpost. One of the native officers suggested that Kabul's brother, who happened to be at the same outpost, kill Kabul so that *badal* was not invoked. Kabul surrendered himself for execution.[162]

The Frontier Corps used similar recruiting methods as the PIF with some important differences. The "divide and rule" method prevailed in the early Frontier Corps. Unlike the Punjab Irregular Force, the Frontier Corps officers recruited with the intention of building mixed companies, a measure that the commanders thought would prevent future rebellions.[163] Both the North and South Waziristan Militias recruited with quotas giving equal representation to tribes on the British side of the frontier and tribes on the far side. In other words, the Afridis and the Wazirs balanced each other in the militia to prevent another mutiny.[164] The militias also created class companies. In the South Waziristan Militia, the units included different classes of Pathans, specifically Khattaks, Afridis, Bangash, and Yasafzais. Major Walter Cummings, a British officer assigned to the South Waziristan Militia, wrote that they also recruited about fifty Wazirs to please the political officers.[165] The exclusion of the Wazirs reflected the fact that the British did not trust them after recent fighting and felt they made poor Soldiers.[166] The South Waziristan Militia had a hard time pacifying its area, partially due to the impact of virtually excluding the Wazirs from military service.

The Frontier Corps underwent a series of reforms to improve the quality of officer assigned to the organization in the 1920s and 1930s to bring it up to the same standard as the PIF. British authorities made service in the corps a major promotional lever for the officers. Service on the frontier also offered officers seeking to make a name from themselves. Officers were seconded from the army to the Frontier Corps for an initial period of three years. Selection required a first-rate evaluation from his regiment, some knowledge of Pushtu. Commanders sought to make selection even more rigorous by administering tests for promotion and retention as a captain.[167] New officers received a significant increase in pay and mileage allowances when they joined the Scouts. Since commanders prohibited new officers from being married, a young officer could save a significant amount of money by serving on the frontier. Even with all the requirement and schooling, one civil servant even remarked that service on the frontier still appealed despite the constant state of fighting because "there were no long hours at the office desk."[168]

British reforms extended beyond improving the selection criteria for the Frontier Corps. Even after the new officer reported to his unit, the officer still had to pass the vetting process to ensure he could function on the frontier, with little guidance and few fellow officers. Once the unit accepted him, he needed to demonstrate mastery of the local language with a few months by passing the Higher Standard Pushtu exam.[169] Finally, newly-assigned officers might have to attend specialized schools that taught the latest frontier tactics.[170]

The Frontier Corps successfully reformed in between the two world wars. By 1924, British officers actively sought a posting to the Corps, and sometimes they returned for two or three tours.[171] The Frontier Corps highlighted the importance of assigning quality trainers to the formation. Massed formations of tribesmen did not mutiny again in the scouts during the interwar period. It is important to note that even after the mutinies in the 1919 campaigns, the British never contemplated ending the practice of using local security units in the North-West Frontier. The units existed, after a series of reforms, until the partition of India and Pakistan in 1947.

Conclusion

The British administration of the NWF and their use of local forces to secure the population has relevance for the modern counterinsurgent. Although the British did not classify any of these missions as a counterinsurgency, they resembled the modern campaigns in Iraq and Afghanistan where aid to the civil power or security of the population also described the mission set.

The British administration based irregular regiments locally and made them answerable to the local administrator. Lord Dalhousie, the Lawrence brothers, and countless other leaders recognized the value of the having a force with knowledge of the local terrain. The units could quickly respond to local emergencies. Additionally, officers trained the units to conduct both civil and military operations. Both the Guides and the PIF remained loyal to the local government through several conflicts, punitive expeditions, and the Indian Mutiny of 1857. During the Mutiny, the reliability of the PIF allowed Sir James Lawrence to quickly secure important government installations in the Punjab. Even when the PIF reverted to the Bengal Army in 1888, another force, the Frontier Corps quickly assumed its role.

The civil and military leaders chose the officers for the irregular regiments because they had the skills deemed necessary for working with indigenous forces. Lawrence chose Lumsden to lead the Guides based on his reputation. The PIF's commander chose the first regimental commandants based on reputation. However, Vaughan suggested that within the first couple of years, a system of removing bad officers from the ranks as a form of self-policing had already developed.[172] Commanders emphasized patience, initiative, physical fitness, and independence when choosing their subordinates. An irregular officer needed these traits because he did have the same number of trained British officers to rely on. Interestingly, knowledge of the local language was not one of the skills necessary for selection as a PIF officer. It was advantageous if the officer did have knowledge of the language used by his troops. However, if Lumsden was a model officer for working with indigenous troops, then he faced a nearly impossible task of learning Pashto, Pukhto, Uzbek, Dari, Persian and a half-dozen other local dialects.[173] Vaughan developed a rudimentary use of the language, but did not formally learn of Pashto until almost twenty years after his command just prior to his return to the area a reporter for the *Times*.[174] Instead officers used the VCOs to communicate with their troops.

The British officers brought a steadying effect to the irregular units, which allowed the government to trust the regiments in situations where their loyalty could be questioned. The militias lacked British officers until Lord Curzon's reforms in 1900. During the Second Sikh War and the Indian Mutiny, units with questionable loyalty were disbanded before they could rebel. However, from 1846-1947 the PIF never had a unit mutiny. The presence of officers is not enough to stabilize all units. The Khyber Rifles were disbanded during the Third Afghan War after the number of desertions reached an alarming rate.

After the Afghan conflict, the Viceroy noted that the quality of the officers assigned to the militias diminished, and he took steps to address the problem. He noted that several junior officers had no frontier experience to compensate for the lower quality recruit in the militias.[175] As a result, the British established a school in Kakul to teach frontier warfare to officers with no experience. The school used experienced officers to teach the drills, training schemes for native troops, and lessons learned in recent operations.[176] Books such as *Passing It On* and *Letters of a Once Punjab*

Frontier Force Officer started to fill doctrinal gap until the military started to produce manuals on mountain warfare.[177] The military also required frontier officers to meet the same promotion and retention requirements as the British Army.

The British system of selection of for service in the PIF and the Frontier Corps not only applied to the officers, but it extended to down to the individual Soldier. The British reinforced the existing class, caste, and tribal system. Although the idea seems contrary to the idea of building a nation-state with a shared identity, it is still practiced in some militaries. The British still recruit the Gurkhas from Nepal for service in the British Army. Many of today's Gurkhas are second-, third-, and fourth-generation Soldiers. The "divide and rule" and martial race theories are probably impossible to implement today when building a new force. The global community would recognize both theories as undermining of the state's security apparatus, and probably racist. Lumsden for example initially recruited the Guides on both a merit basis and tied recruitment to the existing tribal system. The British recognized the importance of honor in the tribal system and used it to their advantage when building security forces. Cummings wrote that VCOs required families and tribes to vouch for new recruits. His experience in the South Waziristan Militia took the reinforcement of tribal system one step further because the commandant could dismiss any Soldier for discipline infraction without referring the issue to the higher commander.[178]

The British officers lived and worked with their irregular Soldiers, sharing both hardship and risk. Men on the frontier constantly faced death. Raiders could overrun an outpost in the night, killing everyone inside. The irregular Soldiers and their officers built trust by sharing the hardship and the threat together. The frontier lacked the comforts of garrison life in one of the bigger garrison cities like Peshawar. Men were not allowed to bring their wives to the frontier garrisons.[179] In the Frontier Scouts, new officers were not allowed to marry during their first tour of duty. One commander even forbade his subordinate officers from taking summers away from the regiment to demonstrate that his officers would share the hardship.[180]

The British assumed risk by stationing so few British Soldiers with the local forces; however, the risk was offset by the benefits local, irregular forces gave to the British administrators. Until trust was built with the Soldiers, the British officers often slept in the same rooms. However, even this practice did not last long.[181] Even following events such as the Indian Mutiny, the Third Afghan War, or even the murder of Captain Bowring, the British never abandoned the practice of using native troops.

Even after disarming the Sikhs, Pathans, and Punjabi Mussalmans after the Second Sikh War, the British had to rely on them during the Indian Mutiny due to the small number of British troops available for the relief of Delhi. However, the native troops provided a local face for the British. They provided invaluable intelligence on the terrain and helped diffuse situations that could have been worse.

However, it is doubtful that politically a modern western power could forcibly place its officers in command of a local security force with the ability to militarily command and control those Soldiers, with all of the subsequent responsibilities including the administration of punishment, without it reeking of a modern day "white man's burden." A modern interventionist power would have to be invited by the indigenous nation's government. A path to transition the security force, such as Indianization, to local control needs to be articulated by the counterinsurgent from the beginning.[182] Another approach to this problem is to build local forces that have both western and local Soldiers initially, and gradually transition it, over time, to the control a local leader.[183] The British did this is a number of places, including British Indian and Oman, through the seconding program with the regular army regiments. Finally, another model is the building of local forces through indirect leadership, the daily mentoring and partnership of western and local forces. This method was how the British trained the *firqat* in Dhofar.

Notes

1. The Raj refers to the period of British administration on the subcontinent. It started with the transfer of rule from the East India Company to the Crown in 1858 after the Indian Mutiny until the partition of India and Pakistan in 1947. It referred to area under direct administration and the princely states that signed treaties with the British government. Richard Holmes, *Sahibs: The British Soldier in India* (London: Harper Press, 2006), 80-81.

2. Colonel J. P. Villiers-Stuart, *Letters of a Once Punjab Frontier Force Officer* (London: Sifton Praed and Co., Ltd., 1925), 1.

3. The British Army refers to the regiments based in Great Britain. Until 1860, the East India Company also maintained an army in India referred to as the East India Company Army. The British Indian Army, or for clarity, the Indian Army refers to the locally recruited regiments in British India, post-1860, with British officers prior to partition in 1947. The distinction is important because Indian Army regiments often deployed from India to fight in a number of imperial conflicts, including Egypt, Abyssinia, East Africa, and the Sultanate of Muscat and Oman. T. R. Moreman, *The Army in India and the Development of Frontier Warfare* (Houndmills: Palgrave, 1998), xx. Tan Tai Yong, *The Garrison State: The Military, Government and Society in Colonial Punjab, 1949-1947* (London: Sage Publications, 2005), 32.

4. *History of the Guides, 1846-1922* (Aldershot: Gale and Polden, 1938), 25.

5. The Punjab Irregular Force's name changed to the Punjab Frontier Force (PFF) by authority of Military Department letter No. 279, dated 19 September 1865. It is also common to see the unit referred to as the Punjab Irregular Frontier Force (PIFF). Members of the unit were referred to as "Piffers." For clarity, the unit is referred to only as the PIF in this study. Colonel H. C. Wylly, *History of the 5th Battalion 13th Frontier Force Rifles* (Eastborne: Antony Rowe Ltd, 1929), 29.

6. Small wars include military action against any body that did not resemble a western army, including native populations and guerrillas. The term included punitive expeditions. Colonel C. E. Callwell, *Small Wars: Their Principles and Practice*, 3rd ed. (London: HM Stationary Press, 1906), 21.

7. Campaigns where civil control of the population does not exist, or has broken down to the extent where the military is the only institution that can provide security. Major General Sir Charles W. Gwynn, *Imperial Policing* (London: MacMillan and Co., Ltd., 1936), 3-4.

8. Campaign where the civil government maintains control, but lacks the personnel numbers to provide adequate security for the populace. The military's duty is to provide assistance for the restoration of law and order during the disturbance. The War Office, *Imperial Policing and Duties in Aid of the Civil Power, 1949* (London: Fosh and Cross Ltd., 1949), 4-5.

9. Moreman, xvii.

10. Field Marshall Roberts, *Forty-One Years in India: From Subaltern to Commander in Chief*, vol. I (London: Richard Bentley and Sons, 1897), 32-34.

11. *History of the Guides, 1846-1922*, 2-3.

12. Tan, 32-33.

13. Holmes, 52.

14. T. A. Heathcote, *The Indian Army* (London: David and Charles, 1974), 14-19, 24-25; Lieutenant General Sir George MacMunn, *The Armies of India* (London: Adam and Charles Black, 1911), 1-37.

15. MacMunn, *The Armies of India*, 5.

16. Moreman, xx.

17. Field Marshal Lord Michael Carver, *The Seven Ages of the British Army* (New York: Beaufort Books. Inc, 1984), 156.

18. Colonel G. J. Younghusband, *The Story of the Guides* (London: MacMillan and Co., 1908), 4-5.

19. Brevet Major General Emory Upton, *The Armies of Asia and Europe* (New York: D Appleton and Co., 1878), 58, 74; Heathcote, 73, 116.

20. For more information on the wars see General Sir Charles Gough and Arthur Innes, *The Sikhs and the Sikh Wars* (London: A.D. Innes and Co., 1897); James Henry Lawrence-Archer, *Commentaries of the Punjab Campaign 1848-49* (London: Wm. H. Allen and Co., 1878).

21. Headquarters, Camp Ferozepore, "Proclamation" (29 March 1849) in James Henry Lawrence-Archer, *Commentaries of the Punjab Campaign 1848-49* (London: Wm. H. Allen and Co., 1878), 253-256.

22. James Lawrence was the brother of Colonel Henry Lawrence. Both were instrumental members of the military and civil service in the Punjab and the NWF. James Lawrence participated in the First Sikh War as commissar for the British Army in the Punjab. After the war, he served as the Commissioner of the Jullundur district under his brother's authority. After the Second Sikh War he joined the Board of Administration for the Punjab. He coordinated the military response in the Punjab at the start of the Indian Mutiny. During the Indian Mutiny he negotiated an agreement with Dost Mohammed Khan, Emir of Afghanistan, to prevent assistance for the insurgents on the frontier. He is credited with moderating the destruction of Delhi during the Mutiny. He served as the Viceroy from 1863-1869. For more information on both brothers see Reginald Bosworth Smith, *Life of Lord Lawrence*, 2 vols. (London: Smith Elder and Co., 1883).

23. Tan, 35-36.

24. Heathcote, 27.

25. "Instructions for the guidance of all officers raising Cavalry and Infantry Regiments of Irregulars in the Punjab" (17 April 1849) in Colonel H. C. Wylly, *History of the 5th Battalion 13th Frontier Force Rifles* (Eastborne: Antony Rowe Ltd, 1929), 2-4.

26. Tan, 36.

27. Villiers-Stuart, 1.

28. Charles Chenevix Trench, *The Frontier Scouts* (London: Jonathan Cape Ltd, 1985), 2; Tan, 37.

29. Trench, xiii.

30. The placement and enforcement of the Durand Line continues to be a problem even today. Afghanistan no longer recognized the Durand Line following the partition of India and Pakistan because it insisted that Pakistan represented a new state. As such, the border between Afghanistan and new state of Pakistan was subject to review. For more information see Bijan Omrani, "The Durand Line: History and Problems of the Afghan-Pakistan Border," *Asian Affairs* 40, no. 2 (2009): 177-195; Thomas Johnson and M.Chris Mason, "No Sign until the Burst of Fire: Understanding the Pakistan-Afghanistan Frontier," *International Security* 32, no. 4 (Spring 2008): 41-77.

31. Major Walter James Cummings, *Memoir of Major Walter James Cummings* (1897-1989) (unpublished) Oriental and India Office Collections (OIOC), British Library (BL), MSS Eur Photo Eur 437.

32. General Sir Peter S. Lumsden and George R. Elsmie, *Lumsden of the Guides: A Sketch of the Life of Lieut.-Gen. Sir Harry Burnett Lumsden, K.C.S.I., C.B., with Selections from his Correspondence and Occasional Papers* (London: John Murray, 1900), 65.

33. Heathcote, 28.

34. Heathcote, 27-29.

35. Moreman, 4-5; Philip Mason in Trench, xiii.

36. This paper does not discuss in depth the various political, economic, and other aspects of the British frontier policies. Instead, the following discussion addresses only the military portion of the British policy.

37. Lal Baha, *NWFP Administration under British Rule 1901-1919* (Islamabad: National Commission on Historical and Cultural Research, 1978), 4-5; Christian Tripodi, *Edge of Empire: The British Political Officer and Tribal Administration on the North-West Frontier, 1877-1947* (Farnham: Ashgate, 2011), 16, 52

38. Trench 2.

39. Tripodi, *Edge of Empire*, 70-71.

40. Tripodi, 72-73.

41. Field Marshal Frederick Sleigh Roberts had the opportunity to observe both the closed border policy and the forward policy. He served most of his career in British India. Roberts commissioned as a Second Lieutenant in the Bengal Artillery while it was still a part of the East India Company Army. He fought in the siege of Delhi and the relief of Lucknow during the Indian Mutiny. He received the Victoria Cross for action at Khudaganj on 2 January 1858. Colonel Roberts commanded the Kurram field force in March 1878. He also fought in the Second Afghan War and served in Afghanistan through the Battle of Kandahar on 1 September 1880.In November 1881 he took over the position of Commander-in-Chief, Madras Army. He ended his career in India as the Commander-in-Chief, India from 1885-1893. His autobiographical *Forty-One Years in India: From Subaltern to Commander in Chief* describes his service in India in detail.

42. Roberts, 32-34.

43. Holmes, 86-87. For more information on the punitive expeditions see Captain H. L. Nevill's *Campaigns on the North-West Frontier* (London: John Murray, 1912) for detailed descriptions of the campaigns.

44. Trench 2-3; Villers-Stuart, 7-9.

45. For more information on the Sandeman system see Christian Tripodi, "'Good for one but not the other'; The Sandeman System of Pacification as Applied to Baluchistan and the North-West Frontier, 1877-1947," *The Journal of Military History* 73, no. 3 (July 2009): 767-802.

46. Moreman, 1-4.

47. Moreman, 23-24.

48. The difference between the words Pukhtun and Pushtun refers to a language and tribal division within the Pathan language. The northeastern tribes speak Pukhto, and the tribes in the southwest speak Pushto. The east- west division is delineated by the Indus just south of Attock through Kohat, up the Miranzi Valley to Thal, and then south of the Kurram River to Hariob and the Shutar-garden pass. One tribe only is split in half between the two, the Khataks. Since most academic discussion defaults to the use of Pushtun, this paper uses it as the default spelling when it is not possible to differentiate between the two languages. Sir Olaf Caroe, *The Pathans* (1958; repr., Karachi: Oxford University Press, 1988), xviii-xix; H. G. Raverty, *A Dictionary of the Pukhto-Pushto or Language of the Afghans* (Ottawa: Laurier Books Ltd., 2001), 330.

49. MacMunn, *The Armies of India*, 148-149.

50. Holmes, 194-195.

51. Trench, 3-4.

52. In Paktia province of Afghanistan the *jirga* has the authority to form an *arbakai* of approximately 2-5 percent of the tribes fighting strength to enforce its decisions. The principle of *badel* does not apply if a member of the *arbakai* kills someone in the execution of his duties. Sherzaman Taizi, *Jirga System in Tribal Life* (Williamsburg: Tribal Analysis Center, 2007), 7.

53. Trench, 3.

54. A *jirga* is "an assembly, a party meets for consultation, a sort of democratic council amongst the Yusufzi's." The tradition is not limited to Yusufzis. The *jirga* is the primary decision making body for both intra- and inter-tribal disputes in the Pushtun society. The most common inter-tribal *jirgas* are formed when feuds erupt the whole fighting strengths of tribes. Under the Frontier Crime Regulations, the British ceded the right to try crimes in the frontier area to the *jirgas*. The *jirga* used Sharia law as the basis of its decisions. If a party violates the decision of a *jirga*, a *lashkar* can be raised to punish the guilty party. Taizi, 6-7; Trench, 7.

55. An irregular force or war party raised by a tribe or tribes to punish the party that violates the decision of a *jirga*, or commits a violation contrary to the *Pukhtonwali* code. Trench.

56. Holmes, 194.

57. Moreman, 12.

58. Colonel George John Younghusband, *Indian Frontier Warfare* (London: Kegan Paul, Trench, Trübner and Co., 1898), 12-13.

59. Temple, 59-60.

60. *History of the Guides, 1846-1922*, 2-3.

61. Heathcote, 27.

62. Younghusband, *The Story of the Guides*, 4.

63. Brigadier W. E. H. Condon, *The Frontier Force Regiment* (Aldershot: Gale and Polden, 1962), 2-3.

64. Lumsden, 66.

65. *History of the Guides, 1846-1922*, 3.

66. Lieutenant Harry Lumsden was actually the Lawrence's fifth choice for the position, behind Lieutenant Prendergast, 8th Cavalry, Lieutenant Pattullo, 1st Fusiliers, and two engineer officers, Lieutenants Beecher and McLagan. The Commander-in-Chief, India approved the release of Pendergast and McLagan to command the cavalry company and the infantry company respectively. He deferred on the appointment of the Commandant, but specified no artillery or engineer officers could be spared. Lawrence appointed Lumsden on 1 December 1846. *History of the Guides*, 3,5.

67. Lumsden and Lawrence were acquainted from a previous assignment. Lumsden accompanied Lawrence's command to Kashmir to assist Maharajah Gulab Singh take possession of the region after its sale from the British. Lumsden also served as a subaltern with 59th Bengal Native Infantry and as a lieutenant in the First Afghan War with the 33rd Native Infantry. Younghusband, *The Story of the Guides*, 3; *History of the Guides, 1846-1922*, 5. For more information on Lumsden's early career see General Sir Peter S. Lumsden and George R. Elsmie, *Lumsden of the Guides: A Sketch of the Life of Lieut.-Gen. Sir Harry Burnett*

Lumsden, K.C.S.I., C.B., with Selections from his Correspondence and Occasional Papers (London: John Murray, 1900).

68. Each irregular regiment had four British officers. The balance of the twenty officers authorized to regiment were native. Tan, 37.

69. Moreman, xxi.

70. Lumsden, 43.

71. The system by which the British determined class, caste, and martial races is a very complex topic. Although MacMunn's writing is one of the earliest attempts to succinctly define them. Also see Heather Streets, *Martial Races: The Military, Race, and Masculinity in the British Imperial Culture, 1857-1914* (Manchester: Manchester University Press, 2004), Tan Tai Yong, *The Garrison State: The Military, Government and Society in Colonial Punjab, 1849-1947* (New Delhi: Sage Publications, 2005), Susan Bayly, "Caste and Race in the Colonial Ethnography of India," in *The Concept of Race in South Asia*, 165-218, ed. Peter Robb, 165-218. (London: School of Oriental and African Studies, 1998); Stephen Cohen, "The Untouchable Soldier: Caste, Politics, and the Indian Army," *Journal of Asian Studies* 28, no. 3 (May 1969): 454; Douglas Peers, "The Martial Races and the Indian Army in the Victorian Era," in *A Military History of India and South Asia*, ed. Daniel P. Marston and Chandar Sundraham (Westport, CT: Praeger, 2007); David Omissi, *The Sepoy and the Raj: The Indian Army 1860-1940* (Basingstoke: Routledge Publishers, 1994) and compare their definitions and discussion of "classes," "castes," martial races and central role of the Punjab in terms of recruitment with Lieutenant General Sir George MacMunn, *Martial Races of India* (London: Low and Marston, 1933).

72. The classes in India do not have social meaning, such as high-class or low-class. Stephen Cohen, "The Untouchable Soldier: Caste, Politics, and the Indian Army," *The Journal of Asian Studies* 28, no. 3 (May 1969): 454.

73. MacNunn, 130-131.

74. MacNunn, 140.

75. The Sikhs require that each member of the sect to take the *pahul*, a form of baptism. A Sikh is not born into the religion like a Christian or Jew. Men aspiring to Sikhism could not join the Indian Army until after they took the *pahul*. MacNunn, 134.

76. Dogras resided in Kangra hills, primarily Rajput, but believed in an orthodox version of Hinduism. David Omissi, *The Sepoy and the Raj: The Indian Army, 1860-1940* (London: MacMillan Press Ltd, 1998), 53.

77. Near the end of the nineteenth century, the British Army discontinued the "divide and rule" practice and started to recruit Soldier based on the martial race theory. The theory postulated that certain races were better suited to discipline, hardship, and soldiering. In some cases the British and the natives agreed. For instance, Rajputs considered themselves a warrior class that gained honor from

killing their enemies. The British divided the different classes in British India into martial and non-martial races. The British sought to exploit inter-tribal rivalry so that different ethnic groups would strive to serve the Raj. The majority of the Soldiers recruited during under the martial race theory were from the yeoman classes. Field Marshal Lord Roberts and Lieutenant General Sir George MacMunn were some of the most active writers in the British India about the martial race theory and its application to the Indian Army. Roberts believed that the lowland tribes were unsuited for military service. The Punjab, on the other hand, produced the best Soldiers. See MacMunn's chapter on the military races of India in *The Armies of India* for his original opinion. Field Marshal Lord Frederick Sleigh Roberts, *Forty-One Years in India: From Subaltern to Commander in Chief*, Vol. II (London: Richard Bentley and Sons, 1897), 441-442; Jeffrey Greenhut, "Sahib and Sepoy: An Inquiry into the Relationship between the British Officers and Native Soldiers of the British Indian Army," *Military Affairs* 48: no. 1 (January 1984): 15-16; Omissi, 20, 25.

78. In fact, Lumsden usually had an excess of men waiting for a vacancy in the Guides. He often had thirty or more replacements around the regiment, paid for by the tribes, waiting for a vacancy. When a spot opened, Lumsden had the replacements shoot for the position. This system gave Lumsden a ready pool of trained replacements that did not cost the government any money to maintain. It also demonstrated the popularity of service in the unit. Younghusband, *The Story of the Guides*, 51-52.

79. David Omissi's study of recruiting in *Sepoy and the Raj: The Indian Army, 1860-1940* suggested that combination of intangible factors like *esprit de corps* and a sense of loyalty compelled Soldiers to serve. Philip Mason agreed with this approach in A *Matter of Honour*. S.P. Rosen believed that Soldiers sought to rise above their caste in a discriminatory society. However, he also suggested that this recruiting strategy helped cause the Indian Mutiny. Finally, Kausik Roy wrote that a combination of the regimental structure reinforced by *esprit de race* allowed the regiments to form distinct identities, which attracted new recruits. Stephen Peter Rosen, *Societies and Military Power: India and its Armies* (Ithaca: Cornell University Press, 1996), 261-262; Kausik Roy, "The Construction of Regiments in the Indian Army: 1859-1913," *War in History* 8, no. 2 (2001): 128-129, 148.

80. Younghusband, *The Story of the Guides*, 53.

81. The initial force included at least Afridis, Gurkhas, Sikhs, Hazaras, Waziris, Pathans, Kafirs, and Yusafzai Soldiers. Lumsden, 66-67.

82. Younghusband, *The Story of the Guides*, 4.

83. Lumsden, 67-69; Younghusband, *The Story of the Guides*, 54-59.

84. This theme of recruiting former enemies as way of simultaneously adding knowledge to the government's forces and denying the same knowledge to the enemy is prevalent in the Dhofar insurgency. Lumsden, 67-73; Younghusband, *The Story of the Guides*, 54-64.

85. *History of the Guides, 1846-1922*, 8.

86. No less a man than Lord Dalhousie praised the Corps of Guides. In September 1847, he wrote to the Guides after the capture of the fort at Govindgarh to thank them for turning the course of the campaign in favor of the government. The guides captured the fort without a shot by disguising themselves as members of the enemy transporting the prisoners. Once inside the fort, they overcame the guards, opened the gates, and allowed the remainder of the guides into the fort. Only a local force could have pulled off the deception successfully. *History of the Guides*, 12-13.

87. *History of the Guides*, 17.

88. Lumsden, 58.

89. Condon, *The Frontier Force Regiment*, 2-3.

90. "No. 754. General Order by the Right Honourable the Governor-General of India" in Colonel H. C. Wylly, *History of the 5th Battalion 13th Frontier Force Rifles* (Eastborne: Antony Rowe Ltd, 1929), 4.

91. The Scinde Camel Corps was designated the 6 Punjab Infantry (Scinde Rifles). The Corps of Guides consisted of one infantry battalion, one cavalry regiment, and a mountain artillery unit. Condon, *The Frontier Force Regiment*, 4; Holmes, 192.

92. The primary difference between the Sind Force and the PIF was its relationship with the army. The Sind Force was part of the Bombay Army, and it took its directions from the Commander-in-Chief, Bombay. Heathcote, 27.

93. "Col S. Black, Secretary to Government Punjab Military Department, to the President Army Organization Commission" (6 September 1879), *Political and Secret Memoranda*, India Office Records (IOR), BL, L/PandS/18/A134; Condon, *The Frontier Force Regiment*, 4.

94. General Sir J. Luther Vaughan, *My Service in the Indian Army – and After* (London: Archibald Constable and Co. Ltd., 1904), 44-45; Holmes, 192-193.

95. Holmes, 197.

96. General Order No. 577, dated 15 February 1851, limited the deployment of PIF to general service in the Punjab and the trans-Indus provinces. It allowed for the deployment out of that region only if "exigencies of the service required it." Wylly, 6.

97. Colonel J. G. Medley, "Defence of the North West Frontier," *Journal of the United Services Institution of India* 9, no. 45 (1880): 288.

98. Moreman, 7.

99. Sir Richard Temple, *Report Showing the Relations of the British Government with the Tribes, Independent and Dependent, on the North-West Frontier of the Punjab from the Annexation in 1849 to the close of 1855* (Calcutta: District Memorandum, 1855), 54, 62. in IOR, BL, V/23/3; Heathcote, 27.

100. General Sir Charles Patton Keyes, "Military Letter from the Government of India, No. 108-933," *Papers of General Sir Charles Patton Keyes (1823-96)* in the Keyes Collection, OIOC, BL, MSS Eur D1084/8.

101. Younghusband, *The Story of the Guides*, 40-43.

102. Wylly, 7.

103. The PIF traced its lineage back to the Frontier Brigade formed in November 1846 with the formation of the first four infantry regiments. The Corps of Guides joined the brigade prior to the Second Sikh War. In 1849, Lord Dalhousie authorized additional units, including artillery, and renamed it the Trans-Frontier Brigade. In 1851, the unit added the Scinde Camel Corps and five regiments of Punjab infantry and took the name, Punjab Irregular Force. Condon, *The Frontier Force Regiment*, 3-4.

104. Each of the presidency armies developed its own recruiting ground, with preferences for caste, class, and religion of their Soldiers. Tan, 32-33.

105. Condon, *The Frontier Force Regiment*, 4; Moreman, 13.

106. Lady MacGregor, ed., *The Life and Opinions of Maj Gen Sir Charles Metcalfe MacGregor*, vol. 1 (London: W. Blackwood and Sons, 1888), 90.

107. Cummings, MSS Eur Photo Eur 437; Moreman, 6.

108. "Instructions for the guidance of all officers raising Cavalry and Infantry Regiments of Irregulars in the Punjab" (17 April 1849) in Colonel H. C. Wylly, *History of the 5th Battalion 13th Frontier Force Rifles* (Eastborne: Antony Rowe Ltd, 1929), 2-4.

109. Moreman, 14.

110. General Sir Samuel James Browne, "Memorandum for Raising Irregular Cavalry, 1855," in the Browne Collection, OIOC, BL, MSS Eur F486/1/1.

111. Moreman, 17.

112. Vaughan, 46-47.

113. Wylly, 11; Cummings, MSS Eur Photo Eur 437.

114. An example of the extent that this personal loyalty went: Lumsden's guides noticed that he was especially sullen after a visit from Sir John Lawrence in 1851. The guides interpreted Lawrence's behavior during the visit as an insult to Lumsden. One remarked, "He starts for Peshawar tomorrow morning there is no reason why he should reach it." Lumsden, 108; Philip Woodruff, *The Men Who Ruled India: Volume II, The Guardians* (London: Jonathan Cape, 1963), 292.

115. The Articles for War did not apply initially because the PIF did not belong to the military. When the Bengal Army absorbed the PIF in 1886, this fact was no longer true, although discipline was never an issue. Vaughan, 47; Cummings, MSS Eur Photo Eur 437.

116. Wylly, 11.

117. "Maj R. C. Lawrence, Secretary to Government, Punjab, Military Department, to Major General R.J. Birch. Secretary to the Government of India Military Department, with the Governor General" (25 October 1859) in IOR, BL, P/191/144.

118. Moreman, 12.

119. The regiments received the order in February 1953 officially changing the service color for the PIF. The 1st Punjab Infantry also had a green uniform for service at the PIF's Headquarters in Peshawar. Younghusband, *The Story of the Guides,* 5; Vaughan, 9, 47; Wylly, 6-7.

120. "Brig.-Gen. A.T. Wilde, Offg. Military secretary to the Government Madras, to the Adj.-Gen." (5 May 1869) in IOR, BL, P/615.

121. Unfortunately this fact had serious ramifications for the regular regiments during a number of punitive expeditions. However, the army never corrected the problem of developing a single doctrine for frontier warfare. In the 1909 edition of *the Field Service Regulations*, the first version printed after the 1897-1898 Frontier Uprising, only had six paragraphs devoted to frontier fighting. Lester W. Grau and Robert H. Baer in General Sir Andrew Skeen, *Passing It On: Fighting the Pushtun of Afghanistan's Frontier* (Fort Leavenworth: Foreign Military Studies Office, 2010), xvii; Moreman, 35, 46.

122. *Brigade Standing Orders issued by the Brigadier General Commanding the Punjab Frontier Force* (6 July 1867) in IOR, P/436/42.

123. Vaughan, 33.

124. Moreman, 27.

125. "Maj R. C. Lawrence, Secretary to Government, Punjab, Military Department, to Major General R.J. Birch. Secretary to the Government of India Military Department, with the Governor General" (25 October 1859) in IOR, BL, P/191/144.

126. Moreman, 21.

127. Moreman, 6. "Watch and ward" is the informal term the Indian Army gave to the frontier duty. It referred to the fact regiments watched the border continuously guarding the population.

128. One example of this was the operations in Bruner in 1897. General Sir Frederick Campbell participated in the campaign as the Commander of the Guides Infantry. He described the use of the Guides infantry throughout the campaign. "Letter to General Campbell from Brig.-Gen. S.F. Crocker" (21 August 1915), Gen Sir Frederick Campbell Collection, LHCMA.

129. Moreman, 45.

130. Several memoirs detail the PIF's role during these punitive expeditions. In addition to the regimental histories, see Forrest's *The Life of Field Marshall Sir Neville Chamberlain* for details of the Umbeyla campaign, Churchill's *The Story*

of the Malakand Field Force: An Episode of Frontier War for the PIF's role in the conflict, and Younghusband's *The Story of the Guides* for details on the Chitral and Malakand expeditions.

131. The Indian Mutiny of 1857 is a watershed moment in the history of British India. As such, several books are needed to explain the origin of the conflict, the military actions of various units, and the results of the conflict. The Mutiny resulted in the Crown assuming control of British India from the East India Company. It also had profound effects on the future recruitment of Soldier from the Punjab. For more information about the Indian Mutiny see William Dalrymple, *The Last Mughal: The Fall of Delhi, 1957* (New York: Bloomsbury, 2006); Lawrence James, *Raj: The Making and Unmaking of British India* (New York: St. Martin's Press, 1997), 233-300. Some of the British officials wrote extensively about their involvement during the Mutiny. See Field Marshall Roberts, *Forty-One Years in India: From Subaltern to Commander in Chief*, vol. I (London: Richard Bentley and Sons, 1897); G. W. Forrest, *The Life of Field Marshall Sir Neville Chamberlain*, (London: William Blackwood and Sons, 1909); Reginald Bosworth Smith, *Life of Lord Lawrence,* 2 vols (London, Smith Elder and Co., 1883). Additionally, *History of the Guides, 1846-1922* of Guides and *The Frontier Force Regiment* histories provide good accounts of the march to Delhi and the Siege of Delhi.

132. Dalrymple, 197.

133. Condon, *The Frontier Force Regiment*, 4.

134. The Guides actually completed the movement in 22 days of marching, with four days of rest and a one-day punitive mission at Kaliran. The regiment's strength actually increased along the march because they added new recruits. Condon, *The Frontier Force Regiment*, 17, 20.

135. Condon, 20-22.

136. Roberts, 253.

137. The future recruitment of Soldiers from the Punjab is a direct result of their loyalty to the British during the Indian Mutiny of 1857. During the mutiny, 14 additional regiments were raised in the Punjab. Recruitment in the Punjab opened to the entire army, which in turn led a disproportionate number of Punjabis under arms in the Indian Army after the Mutiny. Before the mutiny there were only 30,000 Punjabis in the entire army. In June 1858, 75,000 of the 80,000 native Soldiers in the Bengal Army were from the Punjab. 23,000 of them were Sikhs. Rajit Mazumder, *The Indian Army and the Making of the Punjab* (New Delhi: Sapra Brothers, 2011), 11-12.

138. The commission is informally known as the Peel Commission. It differs from the Palestine Royal Commission that considered the changes to the Palestine Mandate in 1936-1937, which was nicknamed the Peel Commission. The commission was comprised of senior civil and military officials with experience in British India. The commission sought to answer twelve questions related to the future organization of the British Indian Army.

139. Philip Mason, *A Matter of Honour: An Account of the Indian Army, its Officers and Men* (London: Papermac, 1986), 225.

140. A British infantry regiment cost 573,343 rupees yearly to maintain. A native infantry regiment cost 277,612 rupees. J. P. Grant "Minute by J. P. Grant, President, Council of India in Council, 4 June 1858," in *Report of the Commissioners Appointed to Inquire into the Organization of the Indian Army; together with Minutes and Appendix* (London: HMSO, 1859), 411.

141. "Precis of Answers Received in India, August 1858," in *Report of the Commissioners,* Appendix 71, 534.

142. Several officials believed after the fact that the reason the Bengal Army overwhelmingly mutinied in 1857 was due to the fact that high-class Hindus were allowed to monopolize military service. As a result the regiments had a shared identity that allowed them to unite against the British officers when presented with a perceived grievance. At the time of the mutiny, Rajputs comprised 34.9 percent of the Bengal Native Infantry regiment and Brahmins comprised 31 percent. Dalrymple, 135.

143. The commission did not recommend the structure of the future army in terms of proportionality of classes in each unit, which classes to include or exclude in the rebuilding of the army. "Testimonies of Sir George Clerk, Governor of Bombay, and Major General Hearsey," in *Report of the Commissioners,* 14.

144. Prior to the Mutiny, each regimental commandant could organize his companies as he saw fit. In the case of the 5th Punjab Infantry, Captain J.L. Vaughan (later General Sir Vaughan) took over a regiment with every class in each of the eight companies. He immediately reorganized the regiment into class companies along the following lines, two companies of Sikhs, two companies of Punjab Mahammedans, two companies of Pathans, one company of Dogras, and one mixed company. Vaughan, 44-45.

145. Tan, 56.

146. Kitchener's reforms of the Indian Army removed the regional nature of the old presidency armies. Now units were eligible for service in anywhere in India. Kitchener's reforms of the British Indian Army reflected a growing awareness of Russia's influence in Afghanistan as part of the "Great Game." Holmes, 196. See Peter Hopkirk's *The Great Game: The Struggle for Empire in Central Asia* (London: John Murray, 1990) for more information on the "Great Game" for control of central Asia between Imperial British and Tsarist Russia.

147. Lumsden opposed this move in writing, arguing that the military would have to create another force to take over the PIF's role. In addition to the PIF answering to the Commander-in-Chief, the Commandant ceased the practice of interchanging infantry and cavalry officers in the Guides. Condon, *The Frontier Force Regiment*, 51-52.

148. Condon, 4.

149. Lord Curzon argued for the establishment of the NWFP following the Frontier Uprising of 1897-1898, stating that the government of the Punjab was inadequate in times of extraordinary circumstances. When that occurred the Government of India needed to be able to exert its power without interference from Lahore. Arthur Swinson, *North-West Frontier* (London: Hutchinson and Co., Ltd., 1967), 259.

150. The Indian Penal Code was the basic criminal law in British India. The Raj implemented it in 1862. Unlike British Common Law it was written. It did not apply in the NWF until after Frontier reforms elevated the NWF's status to a full province. Following the Partition, The Indian Penal Code served as the basis for the Pakistani Penal Code. Trench, 2. For more information on the development of the Indian Penal Code see David Skuy "Macaulay and the Indian Penal Code of 1862: The Myth of the Inherent Superiority and Modernity of the English Legal System Compared to India's Legal System in the Nineteenth Century," *Modern Asian Studies* 32, no. 3 (1998): 513-557.

151. The Frontier Constabulary was an armed police force that worked in the border areas. Swinson, 257; Philip Mason in Trench, xiii.

152. Trench, 8.

153. G. W. Forrest, *The Life of Field Marshall Sir Neville Chamberlain* (London: William Blackwood and Sons, 1909), 474-475.

154. Forrest, 13.

155. Waziristan continues to be a problem for the government of Pakistan to this day. In a 1945 Frontier Committee report, the members noted that the presence of regular troops during the war continued to aggravate the tribes. "Report of the Frontier Committee, 1945," in IOR, BL, L/Mil/17/3/46.

156. Captain H. L. Nevill, *Campaigns on the North-West Frontier* (London: John Murray, 1912), 101, 119.

157. The North and South Waziristan Militias received six British officers each. Trench, 15.

158. Moreman, 99.

159. Moreman, 101.

160. After the resulting punitive expedition in January 1920, Major Cummings troops occupied the same outpost that they destroyed at the beginning of the war. Cummings, MSS Eur Photo Eur 437.

161. The Soldiers of the Khyber Rifles were offered the choice of discharge or transfer to another unit. No native officers opted for discharge, although nearly 80 percent of the Soldiers opted for discharge. They were not reformed until partition in 1947. Trench, 31, 263.

162. Trench, 17-18.

163. Trench, 53.

164. Trench, 15.

165. Cummings, MSS Eur Photo Eur 437.

166. In class breakdowns of the Bengal Army in 1858 and the Indian Army in 1904, the Wazirs are not even listed separately. Omissi, 7, 20.

167. Cummings, MSS Eur Photo Eur 437.

168. Woodruff, 292.

169. Trench, 51-52.

170. The Frontier Corps brought back the mountain warfare schools that had closed following the First World War. Additionally, the Army started to require Frontier Corps officers to meet the same requirements as their comrades in the British Army for promotion and retention. Cummings, MSS Eur Photo Eur 437.

171. Trench, 52.

172. Vaughan, 32.

173. Lumsden, 66.

174. Vaughan, 42.

175. "Chelmsford to Montagu" (8 October 1919) Montagu Collection, OIOC, BL, Mss Eur D523/9.

176. Moreman, 122.

177. Moreman, 171.

178. Cummings, MSS Eur Photo Eur 437.

179. Vaughan, 34.

180. Officers in the regular regiments often moved to higher elevations in the summer to avoid the heat. Few other ranks got the same privilege. The summer period included several of the social obligations, allowed British officers to interact with officers in other regiments, and participate in inter-regimental sports competitions.

181. Vaughan, 38.

182. Indianization refers to the process by which more staff and command positions were offered to native officers. The sacrifices that Indian Soldiers made in World War I accelerated the process. For the first time Indians were allowed to attend Sandhurst to earn a King's or Queen's Indian Officer Commission. The commission was higher than a VCO. See Daniel P. Marston, *Phoenix from the Ashes: The Indian Army in the Burma Campaign* (Westport, CT: Praeger, 2003), 15-17.

183. The US Marines tried this on a limited basis in Vietnam with the Combined Action Platoon (CAP) program. The basic organization of a CAP included one 15-man squad of Marines, a medic, with a 15-20-man unit of the Popular Forces, a local security force. The Marines provided indirect fires, air

support, and training for the PF. The PF provided local intelligence, knowledge of the terrain, and a Vietnamese face for pacification efforts. A Marine squad leader served as the CAP commander, while a PF Platoon Leader served as the unit executive officer. Eventually, CAPs combined to form Combined Action Companies and Combined Action Groups to provide security over larger areas. Michael E. Peterson, *The Combined Action Platoons: The US Marines' Other War in Vietnam* (New York: Praeger, 1989), 136.

Chapter 4

Dhofar

> As our former enemies they knew the ground and the tactics of
> their former friends intimately, and they were good at things that
> we were poor at, namely reconnaissance, gathering intelligence,
> and communicating with the nomadic population. They were of
> that population after all. For all their limitations, I do not believe
> we could have won the war without the *firqat*.
>
> > - Ian Gardiner, *In the Service of the Sultan*

The British experience with irregular security forces did not end
with the partition of India in 1947. Arguably one of the best examples
of an interventionist power building irregular forces to provide security
occurred in the Dhofar province of Oman. The Second Dhofar Insurgency
(1963-1975) provides a different model of partnership for the creation,
mentorship, and employment of local irregular forces to fight in
counterinsurgency operations than the North-West Frontier. Soldiers from
22 Special Air Service (SAS) Regiment, operating under the moniker,
British Army Training Team (BATT), partnered with both singular and
multi-tribal organizations during the conflict. BATT advisors referred to the
local security forces as *firqats*.[1] However, unlike the North-West Frontier,
the SAS troopers did not serve as the officers for the *firqat* units. Instead,
the SAS advised native leaders without actually leading the security force.

Many of 22 SAS Soldiers that operated in Dhofar agree that the *firqat*
did not win the war *per se*, but the *firqat* contributed decisively to the
campaign success.[2] Ian Gardiner, a British Royal Marine seconded to the
Sultan's Armed Forces (SAF), further explained that the *firqat* primarily
provided local security in Dhofar, thereby allowing the SAF to conduct
offensive operations.[3] Furthermore, as with the PIF in the North-West
Frontier, the government eventually absorbed the *firqat* into regular forces.[4]

The British advisors also had another significant advantage during the
insurgency, nearly 160 years of military cooperation between the British
military and the Sultanate. The British recognized the strategic importance
of maintaining good relations with the Sultanate at the end of the 18th
century. In 1798, the British signed a treaty of friendship with the Sultan
of Muscat.[5] The Sultanate represented a point of vulnerability between
Great Britain and British India during the Napoleonic Wars. The initial
treaty prevented French raids on British shipping from bases in Muscat. In
1800, the Royal Navy sent a squadron of ships to the region to assist with

the defense of the Sultanate and other vital interests.[6] British support for the Sultan continued even after the French threat diminished at the end of the Napoleonic Wars.

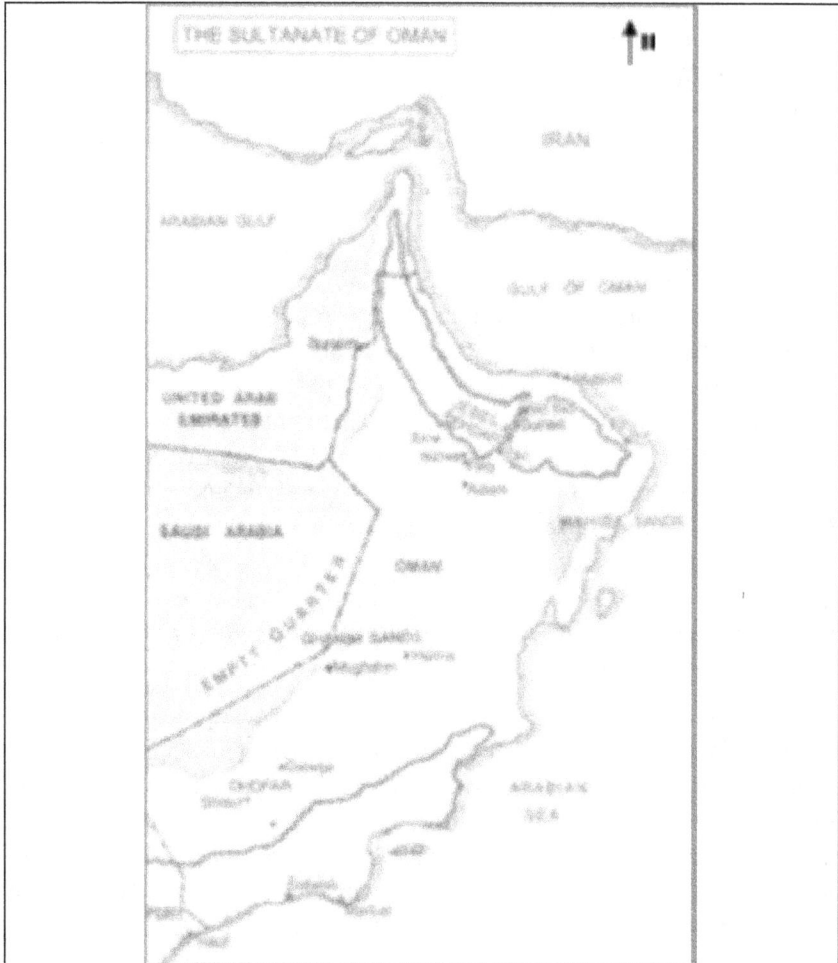

Figure 5. Map of the Oman and the Arabian Peninsula.

Source: Bryan Ray, *Dangerous Frontiers: Campaigning in Somaliland and Oman* (Barnsley: Pen and Sword Military, 2008), 46. CGSC Copyright Registration #12-1353 C/E

The Sultanate included the coast along the Straits of Hormuz, a strategically important waterway in the region. The strait is sufficiently small enough that every ship entering or leaving the Persian Gulf must pass through the Sultanate's territorial waters. Additionally, the Sultanate needed another naval base for the British to protect commercial shipping from India. Since the Sultanate included these strategically important waters, the British continued to provide military assistance to the Sultan to counter Wahabi (Saudi) piracy in the Gulf.[7]

In 1891, the Sultanate received special status within the British Empire, one that remained short of a protectorate, but with significant military benefits. The most significant advantage was the seconding of officers from the Indian Army to the Sultan's militia. Additionally, the Indian Army would provide regiments to reinforce the Sultan's militia in the event of an emergency.[8] By 1913, the Indian Army provided and training for the small force. The British government assisted the Sultanate during the during the 1913 secession crisis with additional troops from British India, money, and military material.[9] Although fighting culminated with the Battle of Bayt al-Falaj in January 1915, the succession crisis officially ended with the Agreement of al-Sib on 26 September 1920. The agreement was significant for two reasons. First, the treaty divided control of Muscat and Oman between the secular Sultan and the religious leader, Imam Salim bin Rashid al-Kharusi. The Imam led the tribes in the Interior (Oman), while the Sultan retained control of the coastal cities (Muscat). Second, it resulted in the creation of the Sultan's Armed Forces (SAF).[10]

The British expanded their military assistance program during the 1930s. First, the British sent a squadron of planes from the Royal Air Force to Oman. The Sultan requested these planes be stationed in Dhofar to assist with policing the troublesome province.[11] By the middle of the twentieth century, the Sultan's Armed Forces (SAF) resembled other British Indian regiments complete with uniforms, standardized authorizations of weapons and equipment, and British officers seconded from the Indian Army.

Over time, the threat to the Sultan's security gradually shifted from Wahabi piracy to territorial disputes with Saudi Arabia. On 12 August 1952, Saudi Arabia seized control of the Burami Oasis. The British initially urged the Sultan to initially limit their response to the Saudi aggression. However after two years of negotiation, with the British government representing the interests of Muscat and Abu Dhabi, and another year in the International Court, the British lent the Trucial Oman Scouts to the Sultan to forcibly eject the Saudis.[12]

In the 1950s, the Imam of the Interior attempted a coup against the Sultan that also required British intervention. After two years of fighting, the First Oman Insurgency stalemated with neither the SAF nor the Imam's forces able to defeat the other. The Sultan asked for British intervention to break the stalemate resulted in the deployment of the 22 SAS Regiment for the first time to the region. Several SAS officers that commanded the regiment, squadrons and troops during the Dhofar insurgency gained experience during this crisis.[13]

By the start of the Second Oman (Dhofar) Insurgency, the British were firmly embedded within the Sultan's regular Armed Forces. A cadre of British officers, including Johnny Watts and Tony Jeapes, had gained invaluable experience in the Sultanate. British military assistance to the Sultan included 150 active duty officers seconded to the SAF (including the SAF commanding officer), 300 contract officers, and up to two squadrons of 22 SAS operating as the British Army Training Team.[14]

Overview of Dhofar Province

Dhofar is the name for the southwest province of the Sultanate of Oman, which borders the eastern edge of the former People's Democratic Republic of Yemen (PDRY). The province is approximately 100,000 square kilometers.[15] Geographically, the province consists of three distinct areas. First, a narrow fertile plain approximately 25 miles long and no more than eleven kilometers wide skirts the southern coastline.[16] The provincial capital, Salalah, and the other principal cities are on the southern plain. Immediately to the north of the fertile plain is a continuous limestone ridge called the *jebel*. The *jebel* rises 1,678 meters from the Indian Ocean.[17] The *jebel* is split in to three regions from west to east, Jebel Dhofar, Jebel Qamar, and Jebel Qara. Numerous north-south wadis intersect the *jebel*. From June until September, the *jebel* is the only portion of the Arabian Peninsula exposed to the southeast monsoon known as the *Khareef*. During this period, the *jebel* is green with vegetation and water runs through most of the wadis. North of the *jebel* is the Empty Quarter Desert, also called the *negd*, which is four hundred miles wide. The desert isolates Dhofar from the rest of Oman. During the insurgency, Dhofar had an estimated population of between 30,000 and 65,000. Of those, approximately two-thirds lived on the fertile plain, and one-third lived in the *jebel*.[18] A single road, the Midway Road, connects Dhofar with the rest of Oman. The geography is significant to military operations, because a commander could find his unit fighting in three different geographical zones, desert, mountains, and dense vegetation, on the same day despite the fact that different types of uniforms and equipment were needed in each region.[19]

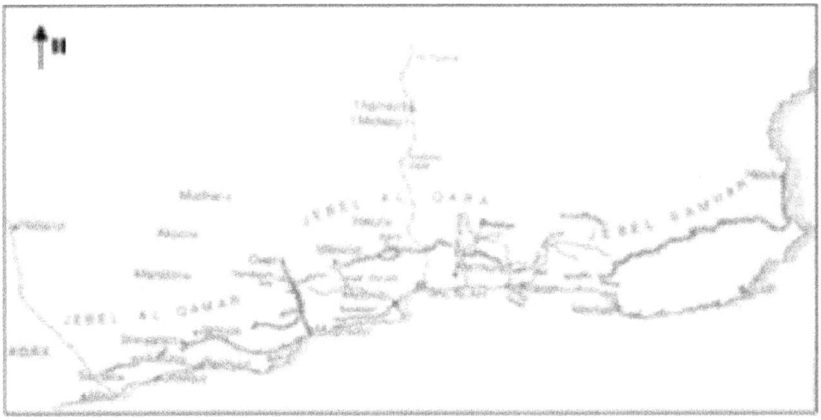

Figure 6. Map of Dhofar.

Source: Bryan Ray, *Dangerous Frontiers: Campaigning in Somaliland and Oman* (Barnsley: Pen and Sword Military, 2008), 58. CGSC Copyright Registration #12-1353 C/E

Dhofar's isolation from the rest of Oman is important for two reasons. First, the Dhofaris are ethnically different from the northern Omanis. Most Omanis physically and culturally resemble Arabs and speak Arabic as their primary language. However, the Dhofari people are ethnically related to Ethiopians and Somalis rather than Arabs. The Dhofaris share cultural characteristics with the Somalis, including the pride in their cattle, the design of their round stone and straw houses, and stance.[20] Omanis traditionally speak Arabic; however, Dhofaris speak a local, glottal dialect referred to as *Jebali* or *Harasis*, both of which are closer to Aramaic than Arabic linguistically.[21] Finally, Dhofar's society is tribal-centric. Several observers, both civil and military, noted that a Dhofari's allegiance is to his herd, followed by his family, and tribe. Islam is fourth on his list. The Dhofari did not owe allegiance to a distant master, the Sultan, or an artificial state that did not understand his society.[22] The isolation prevented assimilation of the Dhofari culture with the larger Omani culture.

Second, Dhofar's isolation ensured its relative independence with the Sultanate. Historically, Dhofar operated as a separate entity since Sultan Al Bu Said first annexed it in 1829. The province did not come under the Sultan's control until an expedition occupied Salalah in 1879.[23] The province has the traditional governance structure of the other provinces, with a *wali* appointed by the Sultan as the governor of the province. However, unlike other provinces, Dhofar's *wali* reported directly to Said, making him equal to the Interior Minister. The Dhofar also issued its own coinage prior to 1970.[24] Furthermore, the Sultan differentiated Dhofar from the rest of the provinces, because he believed that the province was his personal property.[25] Said took both his first and second wives from the powerful Bait Mashani tribe in Dhofar.[26] In 1958, he established permanent residence in his Dhofar palace.

Social Conditions in Dhofar

In order to ensure that Oman remained firmly under his control, Sultan Said bin Taimur imposed strict restrictions on modernization to control the population. He inherited the Sultanate of Muscat and Oman following his father's abdication in 1932.[27] The Sultan associated modernization with radical behavior.[28] He restricted travel outside the country and movement within the country. Two hospitals, one operated by American missionaries located in Matrah and another operated by the British consulate located in Muscat, provided the only modern health care in Oman.[29] The Sultan enacted laws to prohibit any outward signs of modernization such as spectacles, radios, flashlights, gas stoves, and automobiles. In 1952, only two official automobiles existed in the country, one for the Sultan's use and one for the British consul. The only paved road in the country connected the Sultan's palace in Muscat to the airport.[30] Education also remained primitive even for Middle East standards of the time. Females attended school until age 12 and males until age 22. Education was a community responsibility with a focus on memorization of the Koran. Said restricted higher education to only three state-run schools.[31] Despite these restrictions, Said secured British recognition of Oman's independence in 1951.[32] He continued to refuse to modernize the country even after the successful exploration and extraction of oil brought the country additional revenue in 1964.

The Dhofaris especially suffered under the Sultan. He likened Dhofaris to a bunch of cattle thieves.[33] He used to tell his British advisors that if they encountered a snake and a Dhofari at the same time, step on the Dhofari because he presented a greater threat.[34] The Sultan instituted a series of social changes to control the population. Dhofaris had to live day-to-day without the possibility of gaining wealth. Dhofar used to be a region rich in crops. Prior the First World War, the Salalah Plain served as the breadbasket of Mesopotamia (Iraq). During the war, the region produced enough grain to feed all of the British Middle Eastern forces. When Said took control of the country, he started to cap water wells and destroy the old system of aqueducts that channeled water from the *jebel* onto the plain limiting the Dhofaris' ability to grow crops and increasing their dependence on livestock.[35]

In addition to his population control measures, Said prohibited the Dhofaris from joining the security forces. The Sultan believed that by not arming and training the Dhofaris, he could prevent a future rebellion. As a result, several Dhofaris left the country to join the British-officered Trucial Oman Scouts in the future United Arab Emirates.[36] These foreign-trained Dhofari served as the military backbone of the Dhofar Liberation Front (DLF).[37]

The ethnic differences between the Dhofaris and the Omanis made policing tough in Dhofar. The Dhofaris viewed the Omani and Baluchi[38] security forces as interlopers.[39] As a result, the Dhofaris and the security forces never built a level of trust needed to fight a counterinsurgency. For a short period of time, Sultan Said relied on a local, irregular unit "The Dhofar Force" to police the violence in the province.[40] This unit rarely numbered more than 60 men at any given time, and never controlled the rising levels of violence because of their small numbers. However during a military parade in Salalah in 1966, two members of the Dhofar Force attempted to shot the Sultan at close range. The assassination attempt confirmed his fears about the Dhofaris, and he reorganized the unit using only former slaves.[41]

First Oman Insurgency

After twenty years of ruling the Sultanate with draconian laws, Sultan Said was extremely paranoid about rebellion. He used his powers of imprisonment to dissuade dissent.[42] Although he firmly controlled the coastal cities, he remained suspicious of the tribes. He technically still shared power with the Imam of the Interior as per the 1920 Agreement of al-Sib. In 1954, Imam Muhammad bin Abdullah died resulting in another succession crisis similar to the one that occurred in 1913. Ghalid bin Ali assumed the position as the Imam of the Interior, but he lacked popular tribal support. Aided by Saudi Arabia and Egypt, Ghalid attempted to establish an independent imamate to consolidate his power with the interior tribes.[43] His actions quickly resulted in the First Oman Insurgency.[44] The Sultan's forces quickly defeated Ghalid's followers and placed Ghalid in house arrest. Said abolished the power sharing arrangement and personally received the allegiance of several of the interior tribal sheikhs.[45]

The Sultan originally believed that the rebellion had passed without a serious threat to his rule. However Ghalid's brother, Talib bin Ali, escaped to Saudi Arabia and established a training camp for rebel fighters. Two years later in May 1957, Talib's Liberation Army of about 100 fighters returned to Oman with the intent of establishing a separate imamate. Talib's forces recruited some of the most powerful tribes in the interior. The Sultan attempted to defeat the insurgency with his military. However, the SAF lost the initial battles at Balad Sait and Nizwa on 13-15 July, 1957.[46]

Sultan Said believed that the Liberation Army posed a serious threat to his rule following the SAF's defeat in the initial battles. He turned to the British government for assistance. Later in July 1957, a hastily assembled British and SAF force defeated Talib's troops in Nizwa.[47] The Liberation Army survivors retreated to the Jebel Akhdar where they remained throughout 1958. During the pause in 1958, the Jebel Akhdar obtained an almost mystic reputation. Omanis started to believe that the mountain was impenetrable. The British sent the SAS to Oman in December 1958 to assist the SAF with an assault of the Jebel Akhdar. In January 1959, the SAS, SAF, and elements of the Life Guards assaulted the *jebel* and dislodged the remainder of Talib's army. Both Johnny Watts and Tony Jeapes commanded SAS troops during the operation. Again, the survivors fled to Saudi Arabia.[48] The fact that the SAS and SAF climbed the mountain in one night broke the spirit of the rebellion. Some of the survivors combined with other Dhofaris to form the DLF.

The Dhofar Insurgency

The Dhofar Insurgency materialized in response to Sultan Said's harsh treatment of the Dhofaris. The Dhofaris grew disenchanted with the Sultan's harsh methods of control, unwillingness to modernize, and his constant paranoia toward the tribes. Disillusioned Dhofaris sought to establish an independent Dhofari state.

Initially, the insurgent movement started slowly because they lacked political and military organization. The first attack occurred in April 1963 when insurgents attacked a number of John W. Mecom Oil Company vehicles traveling on the Midway Road.[49] However, the SAF did not pursue the rebels while the insurgency struggled to organize.[50] Within two years, the unorganized independence movement grew into a full insurgency. By 1965, the insurgents organized into a political body, the DLF, and military formation, the Dhofar Liberation Army (DLA). The rebels sought and received support from Saudi Arabia, Syria, Libya, Egypt, and Iraq.[51] At the same time, the SAF started to keep a company-sized element in Dhofar. For the next two years the DLA and the SAF fought a series of tit-for-tat operations. Typically, the DLA conducted small-scale harassment attacks against the SAF and the Dhofar Force, and the SAF responded to these attacks with company-sized search-and-destroy missions. Additionally, the Sultan stepped up punitive measures including the capping of water wells, further destroying the Dhofaris' way of life. Surprisingly, the search-and-destroy missions were effective at killing and capturing insurgents. In fact, the SAF had nearly militarily defeated the DLA by December 1967, but the Sultan failed to realize that the SAF's missions added to the Dhofaris' sense of discrimination, and they started to push the populace toward supporting the insurgency.[52]

The SAF's momentum against the DLA reversed suddenly at the end of 1967. The officers noticed that the insurgents increasingly had access to modern weapons, vehicles, and equipment. Additionally, the enemy started to maneuver like a military unit.[53] The sudden change coincided with the completion of British withdrawal from Aden and South Arabia, later the People's Democratic Republic of Yemen to the west of Oman on 29 November 1967.[54] The British had fought a bitter and ultimately unsuccessful counterinsurgency against the National Liberation Front (NLF) and the Front for the Liberation of Occupied South Yemen (FLOSY). Despite the British offer of future independence in 1968, the NLF and FLOSY continued to fight the British troops stationed in the country. The British counterinsurgency effort lacked accurate intelligence on their opponents. Frustrated by a lack of progress and the mutiny of Arab Soldiers during the Six Day War, the British government announced a timeline for the withdrawal of all British forces. In 1969, FLOSY defeated the NLF in a brief civil war and the established a Marxist state, the People's Democratic Republic of Yemen (PDRY).[55]

The British withdrawal from Aden in 1967 changed the course of the Dhofar insurgency. Whereas the SAF had previously received support from British Forces in Aden, Dhofar now bordered a state openly hostile to the Sultanate.[56] The PDRY communists declared their intent to spread communism throughout the Persian Gulf region, and they offered DLF insurgents sanctuary just across the border.

The Dhofari insurgents took advantage of the sanctuary to reorganize their forces and clarify their objectives. In 1968, the communist-aligned Popular Front for the Liberation of the Occupied Arabian Gulf (PFLOAG) replaced the DLF and assumed control of the insurgency. PFLOAG received support from China, and Chinese-trained political officers gradually infiltrated Dhofar to indoctrinate the *jebeli* tribes.[57] The communist indoctrination process was also brutal at times. The communists sent children across the border to Hauf for reeducation, suppressed Islam and the tribalism, and mandated support for the hard-core communist fighters.[58]

PFLOAG's military organization and operations also benefited from Chinese assistance. The insurgents divided Dhofar into three regions with a military unit assigned to operate in each region.[59] The *adoo*[60] or enemy, conducted operations with the intent of severing SAF control of the Midway Road, further isolating Dhofar and limiting the SAF's ability to conduct operations on the *jebel*. The SAF gradually evacuated the garrisons in the coastal towns of Mirbat, Sudh, and Rakyat and surrendered control of the coastal highway to the insurgents. By 1970, the government of Oman barely controlled the provincial capital, Salalah.[61]

In January 1970, the SAF conducted an internal assessment of the counterinsurgency operation in an attempt to understand why the counterinsurgency strategy was failing. The assessment relied heavily on counterinsurgency lessons learned in Kenya, Malaya, and Aden. They cited many shortcomings with the Sultan's strategy mostly related to the fact that the Sultan failed to create a holistic program that addressed the underlying social issues. The SAF's objective remained purely military, specifically to kill the enemy.[62] The Dhofaris, when given the chance to choose between the Sultan's harsh methods and the communist's harsh methods, chose the communists.

In June 1970, another communist-backed group, the National Democratic Front for the Liberation of Oman and the Arabian Gulf led a coup attempt in northern Oman. The SAF quickly defeated it, but the attempt demonstrated the Sultan's unpopularity in the entire country, not just Dhofar. Said could no longer claim that the problem centered on the uncivilized Dhofaris.

In the end, Said's paranoia was founded, although the tribes were not the group that finally challenged his power. A bloodless palace coup deposed the Sultan on 23 July 1970. His son Qaboos bin Said assumed control of the country. Qaboos had studied at Sandhurst and served with the British Queen's Own Cameron Highlanders regiment in Germany. During his education, he toured Great Britain to learn about local governance. Both his studies and his military experience exposed him to western ideas.[63] When Qaboos returned to Oman, he recognized that the Omanis, and especially, the Dhoraris had legitimate grievances. His father recognized that Qaboos presented a threat, and he placed Qaboos under house arrest, limited his involvement in the government, and censored his mail. Qaboos was only allowed to study the Koran and Omani history.[64]

The coup served as the second turning point in the war. Qaboos's installment as the Sultan gave the British civil advisors and military officers in the Sultanate the opportunity to change the course of the counterinsurgency campaign. Within days, Qaboos announced and instituted a series of social reforms in Oman with the objective of addressing legitimate social grievances. In Dhofar these reforms included improved education, employment, amnesty, and access to water for the cattle. Additionally, Qaboos recognized Dhofar as the southern province of Oman, equal to all other provinces in the Sultanate.[65] The new Sultan also proclaimed a general amnesty for any *adoo* that gave up resistance. The non-committed remnants of the DLF, including Salim Mubarak, the leader of the first *firqat*, took advantage of the amnesty offer and moved off the *jebel*. Qaboos promised a military campaign to remove the communist elements in Dhofar.[66]

BATT Plan for Dhofar

Within days of the coup, a group of Soldiers from 22 SAS Regiment arrived in Dhofar to assist the new Sultan with his counterinsurgency plan. The SAS arrived ready to implement a pre-approved five-point counterinsurgency plan. In March 1970, before the coup, Lieutenant Colonel Johnny Watts, the 22 SAS CO and a veteran of the earlier insurgency, came to Dhofar and conducted his own assessment of the counterinsurgency. Upon conclusion, he advised Brigadier John Graham, Commander Sultan's Armed Forces (CSAF), of his plan. Watts stressed that any SAS involvement was a short-term, stopgap measure to allow the Sultan time to implement social reforms. The Sultan and Omanis had to provide the long-term solution to address the insurgency. Watts briefed Graham a five-front plan called *Operation Storm* to fight the insurgency:

1. A medical campaign to provide basic medical and dental care to the Dhofaris, including those living on the *Jebel*.

2. A veterinary campaign to increase agricultural yields and provide fresh water for the Dhofaris' livestock.

3. An organized intelligence operation.

4. An information campaign designed to counteract Communist propaganda and to persuade the rebels to change sides.

5. The recruitment and training of Dhofari Soldiers to fight for the Sultan.[67]

Graham adopted all five points and published on 20 November 1970 as part of Plans 7 codifying the military's role in Dhofar. Plans 7's mission statement for all of the military forces in Dhofar simply read, "to end the rebellion in Dhofar." In the summary of tasks to government forces and agencies, the task of selecting and training irregular *jebeli* forces is mentioned in writing for the first time. Later in the order, the CSAF tasked the BATT specifically with raising and training of local auxiliary troops and advising the CSAF on the mounting of irregular operations using those units.[68] Watts returned to Great Britain to brief the SAS on their new mission.

After Watts returned to Hereford, he issued his guidance to D Squadron, commanded by Major Tony Jeapes, another veteran of the earlier insurgency. First, Jeapes's primary objective was to give Qaboos time to enact social programs to address the Dhofaris grievances by preventing the spread of the insurgency. Second, the squadron could not take casualties. Finally, Jeapes had no obligation to report his progress back to the United Kingdom because of an agreement between Queen's government and the Sultan. This final point effectively gave Jeapes a free hand to prosecute the campaign without the British government interfering. However, this agreement was a two-edged sword. Jeapes could expect little to no assistance from the United Kingdom in terms of additional men or material.[69]

Although Jeapes would not receive assistance from Hereford, he did bring additional manpower. The first group of SAS Soldiers that arrived in September 1970 lacked the manpower to conduct the irregular forces mission while simultaneously starting work on the other four tenets of Watts's plan. When Jeapes's D squadron arrived in January 1971, the focus shifted to creating the *firqat*.

The first group had identified a possible leader for the *firqat*, Salim Mubarak. Mubarak's group presented themselves to the BATT's advance party two days prior to the arrival of Jeapes's troop. According to one of the BATT Soldiers present, no one was knew what to do with the group of former insurgents. The fact that former insurgents wanted to suddenly fight for the Sultan was an unintended effect of the amnesty offer. A BATT Arabic linguist and a SAF intelligence officer talked with Mubarak throughout the first night to establish his intentions and sincerity. He told the BATT that he previously fought the SAF as the DLF's second in command of Eastern Area. He took advantage of the Qaboos's amnesty offer and now wanted to raise his personal standing as the commander of new local security force. Mubarak came from a minor tribe, and his motivation for forming the *firqat* also included the personal aspect of raising his position and that of his tribe.[70]

After the BATT established Mubarak's sincerity, the group met with Jeapes and pitched a plan for the formation of multi-tribal irregular force called the Firqat Salahdin. Mubarak envisioned that the Firqat Salahdin would consist of a thousand Soldiers fighting the communists from one side of the *jebel* to the other.[71] The two men decided to form the Firqat Salahdin from Mubarak's group of former insurgents that had surrendered following Qaboos's amnesty offer.[72]

After meeting with Mubarak, Jeapes needed to pitch the idea of using former insurgents to form the *firqat* to Graham. Jeapes stressed that the *firqat* must be armed with the same weapons as the SAF and trained in the use of mortars and machine guns by the BATT. He also reiterated that for the *firqat* to be a legitimate fighting force, Graham must command them. Graham questioned Jeapes on the risk of forming a force that could defect at any moment, given that most of the men had previously fought against the SAF earlier in the insurgency. In the end, the CSAF consented to the formation of the *firqat*s, and requested additional SAS Soldiers from the United Kingdom to supplement the mission.[73] The task of raising the *firqats* had finally developed into its own operation, *Operation Emu.*[74]

Recruitment

Before the *firqat* could take over the local security mission, the BATT needed to recruit and train the locals. Mubarak's group of SEPs formed the core of the Firqat Salahdin. The use of SEPs for the *firqats* is an ingenious method of depriving the enemy of resources, while addressing one of primary grievances of the Dhofaris in the process. Killing an *adoo* simply deprived the enemy of one Soldier. However, by recruiting a SEP into the *firqat*, the counterinsurgent has changed the balance of power by two. He added one additional Soldier to his formation, while depriving the enemy of a Soldier. Additionally, the use of SEPs for local security undermined one of the DLF's original propaganda messages, "Dhofar for the Dhofaris."[75] *Firqats* made Dhofaris stakeholders in their own security, an option that they were not offered by Sultan Said. Finally, a living SEP fighting in the *firqat* had psychological value. He talked to his relatives, including sometimes the ones fighting with the *adoo*, and relayed the Sultan's messages.[76]

The SEPs in the Firqat Salahdin were unique, because they belonged to several different tribes, some of them rivals. Mubarak argued that tribal dynamics were not important in forming the *firqat*. He believed that since the communists formed their units without regard for tribal structure, that the government could also form units from several tribes. However, this belief ignored two different important facts about the Dhofari tribal system. First, every man, regardless of position, wealth, and class, is equal. The *firqat* elected two leaders, one to command military operations and a tribal leader to decide political issues.[77] If a man disagrees with the leader's decision, he is not obligated to follow the orders. This tribal caveat complicated the training and employment of the *firqats*. Later attempts to impose a rank structure, chain of command, and uniforms failed.[78] Jeapes believed that Mubarak wanted a multi-tribal structure to the Firqat Salahdin to counteract this problem.[79] The second thing that Mubarak's believe ignored is the fact that if the BATT used the same coercive methods that PFLOAG used to integrate the communist units, then it would undermine the other four tenets of Watts's plan.

However, the tribal system also benefitted the BATT when it came to recruiting tribesman for the *firqats*. The tribes viewed each other as rivals. Once one tribe formed a *firqat* and reaped the benefits of working with the Sultan, then the neighboring tribes wanted to create a *firqat*. Shortly after Mubarak approached Jeapes about the formation of the Firqat Salahdin, the Bait Kathir approached Jeapes about forming their own tribal *firqat*. The Bait Kathir was one of the largest tribes on the *jebel*. Additionally, the tribe's fighters formed the core of the insurgency before the communists started to support the PFLOAG.[80] The tribal model prevailed throughout the remainder of the war.[81]

Training

The fact that the tribes quickly changed to the Sultan's side and each one wanted to form their own tribal *firqat* presented the new series of problems for the BATT. Even after the arrival of additional SAS Soldiers from Great Britain, the BATT could not train the *firqat* quickly enough. No curriculum existed for training the Dhofari tribesmen. The BATT advisors saw quickly that each tribe had its own personality, and they quickly discovered that no two *firqats* could be trained exactly the same. For instance, the Firqat Salahdin completed trained quickly because it had fought together against the SAF on the *jebel*. Jeapes gave the BATT advisors a desired end state and allowed them to assess the *firqatmen's* individual skills. The BATT advisors initially trained the *firqatmen* in weapon handling, basic tactics, first aid, and the use of explosives.[82] The BATT quickly discovered that the *firqat* could shoot accurately over long distances, and the *firqatmen* actually maneuvered better the BATT Soldiers on the *jebel*. The average Dhofari that joined the *firqat* had some military experience with the adoo, but more importantly, he had walked the land with his cattle since he was boy.[83] Interesting, the *firqats* also asked the

BATT to incorporate drill periods into the training because the leaders felt it increased individual discipline.[84]

The amount of time the BATT spent training a *firqat* depended on the pace of operations. If the *firqat* was needed for a mission in a certain tribal area the training might consist of only a week of training. Ideally, the training consisted one week of administrative work followed by a month of training, although even this timeline was subject to pace of operations.[85] The training consisted of weapons training (to include maintenance) and qualification to 800 meters, tactics, fire and movement, use of terrain, ambush drills, patrolling, first aid, and drill. Secondary subjects included the use of radios, mortar fire control, and a demonstration of close air support.[86] By all accounts, the *firqatmen* had a good understanding of fire and maneuver from their previous *adoo* experiences or in some cases with *jebeli* tribes, raiding rival tribes. The primary area of instruction was on use of the FN rifle versus the AK-47.[87]

The tribal structure of the *firqats* actually made training more efficient for the BATT over time. As SEPs indicated their desire to join the *firqat*, they were welcomed into their tribal unit. The veteran members of the *firqat* quickly trained the new Soldier in weapon handling, maneuver, and their responsibilities in the *firqat*. In effect, this method treated the new Soldier as a replacement, rather than a new Soldier, and the BATT did not have to establish a permanent training facility solely for purpose of training new *firqatmen*. This fact that most SEPs already had some form of military training in another regional unit such as the Trucial Oman Scouts or from PFLOAG allowed for this method of training new Soldiers to succeed. It probably could not have worked if the *firqatman* did not have the necessary background skills.[88] Additionally, the tribal nature of the *firqat* allowed for the *firqat* leaders to vouch for SEPs, take responsibility for their actions, and immediately welcome them to the unit.[89] A SEP usually knew multiple members of the *firqat* upon his arrival.

Partnership

Partnership between the BATT and the *firqat* on operational missions proved equally important to the success of initial operations, both to establish trust between the units and for the *firqat* to build confidence in their skills. Once the BATT finished initial training of each *firqat*, a four-Soldier team from the troop that trained the *firqat* remained with the organization during operations.[90] The BATT element lived within the *firqat* defensive lines when they conducted missions. Additionally, the BATT provided the General-Purpose Machine Gun (GPMG) and mortar support, and provided the air ground liaison with SOAF during *firqat* operations.[91]

The BATT advisors seemed to partner well with the *firqat*. The BATT was used to working with irregular Soldiers through unconventional means. However, both BATT and SAF veterans agree that a special type of personality was needed to work successfully with the *firqat* in the long-term. The veterans interviewed agreed that the Soldiers that were successful in working with the *firqats* shared a number of characteristics including patience, good attitude, reliability, a sense of humor, and physical fitness.[92] Additionally, the trainer needed to genuinely care about his *firqat* and advocate for them with the SAF and the BATT commander. However, the trainer needed to be careful not to try to "go native" since the *firqat* would consider that action disingenuous.[93] Finally, one BATT commander suggested that exposure to other cultures prior to arriving in Oman assisted trainers, because those trainers seemed more receptive to different cultural norms.[94]

Trust between the *firqat* and the embedded BATT Soldiers never seemed to be an issue during operations after the period of adjustment. The BATT initially kept a guard during the night, not so much against the *adoo*, but against the *firqatmen*. The *firqat* were almost entirely turned *adoo*, and there was no guarantee that with the right motivation, the *firqatmen* could rebel, kill the small BATT element, and take their weapons over to the *adoo*. For the same reason, each BATT advisors also initially carried a sidearm for personal protection. Despite this ease by which this scenario could occur, there are no reports of a *firqatman* killing or wounding a member of the BATT, SAF, or even the Iranian Soldiers.[95] Over time, this relationship of mutual suspicion disappeared.

Initial Operations

The BATT also quickly learned during the initial operations that the *firqat* had considerable strengths as an irregular security force. The *firqatmen* know the terrain a better that the SAF or the BATT. They spoke the local dialect, and they understood the *jebeli* tribal dynamics. Most importantly, the *firqats* gathered intelligence by talking to the populace better than any other fighting unit.

Jeapes considered the Firqat Salahdin a good fighting unit, and he assigned them the hardest missions even after other tribal *firqat*s completed their training. Jeapes also realized that the Firqat Salahdin needed an easy first victory to prove the concept of local indigenous forces in Dhofar. Mubarak's personal pride and pride in the Firqat Salahdin might have prompted him to choose a mission that exceeded the capabilities of the unit. Jeapes needed an easy victory to reinforce his talking points with the

CSAF that the *firqat* were an important piece to defeating the insurgency. Ideally, the *firqat* could provide the manpower and local expertise that the SAF and the BATT lacked. Jeapes decided to conduct this operation against the fifty-*adoo* fighters in the coastal town of Sudh. Finally, Sudh represented the easternmost influence of the insurgency and that made reinforcement during the attack unlikely.[96]

At 0100 hours on 24 February 1971, the Firqat Salahdin landed on the beach outside of Sudh. At 0630, the *firqatman* and BATT advisors quickly secured the town and the key infrastructure, a government fort in the town's central square. Mubarak quickly raised the Sultan's flag over the fort and yelled out a pro-government message. Over the course of the day, the *firqat* secured the town, engaged the male population, and located the *adoo*. Within two days, the operation resulted in the defection of the *adoo* leader, Mohammed Qartoob, and sixteen of his subordinates. An additional 36 *adoo* surrendered later the same day. Many of these SEPs, including Qartoob, eventually joined the *firqat*. The entire operation resulted in no casualties and no shots fired. Jeapes and several other BATT advisors accompanied the mission, but they allowed Mubarak and the other *firqatmen* to execute the mission. Mentorship in this case consisted primarily of providing resources and ensuring that the mission planned did not exceed the capabilities of the Firqat Salahdin.[97]

Problems with the *Firqat*

The *firqat* were not a perfect organization even with their BATT partners. Advisors recommended the allocation of plenty of time to negotiate the timing and scope of the operation with the *firqat*. Another consideration unique to raising tribal forces is the tribal dynamics of the culture. The *firqat* routinely refused to operate outside of the tribe's territory. This problem was especially frustrating to the BATT during operations that crossed tribal boundaries. In some cases, the *firqat* leader could stop, point a spot on the ground, and state that his men could go no further, because he had reached the edge of his tribe's land. Additionally, the *firqat* would also stop assisting an operation in the middle of a firefight. The BATT usually speculated that one of the *firqatman* had spotted a relative or another member of his tribe in the *adoo* unit they were fighting.[98] The *firqat's* problems are not without merit. Aside from possibly fighting against one's brother, cousin, etc., the *jebeli* tribes still believed in and occasionally enforced blood feuds.[99]

Again, the Firqat Salahdin had problems associated with it due to its unique tribal structure. Ultimately, the multi-tribal structure proved unsuccessful. Mubarak died unexpectedly from a heart attack, leaving the *firqat* without a strong leader. The man chosen to succeed Mubarak, Mohammed Said, belonged to minor tribe, the Bait Gatun. However, another leader in the *firqat*, Qartoob (the former *adoo* commander in Sudh), belonged to the more powerful Bait Umr tribe. Jeapes learned that Qartoob and his twenty Soldiers would not serve under Said's leadership. Jeapes appealed to their pride and required the men to quit the *firqat* during a morning parade. Most of the 65 men quit to join other tribally based *firqats*.[100] Thus, the Firqat Salahdin ceased to be a unit on 23 April 1971, less than three months after their formation.[101] Jeapes assessed that this method did not work as well as basing the *firqat* on tribal lines based on his observations of other *firqat* currently in training. He did not attempt to form another tribally heterogeneous formation during the rest of his command.

Operating with SAF

The problems with the *firqat* extended beyond the relations with their BATT advisors. The SAF and the *firqat* operated together on the *jebel* for most missions; however, the two organizations merely tolerated each other's presence. The SAF resented the loose discipline in the *firqat*. The *firqat* never organized into standardized formations with a distinct chain of command, which caused the BATT to serve as an intermediary between the SAF and the *firqat*. Gardiner referred to them as volatile, argumentative, unpredictable, and grasping.[102]

The *firqat's* indiscipline also caused consistent supply issues. If a *firqatman* were issued four bottles of water in preparation for an operation, he would drink it prior the start of the mission. If the *firqatman* was not thirsty, he would use the to wash during a mission. When the BATT advisor questioned the *firqat* commander, the advisor received a response along the lines of "if Allah wants us to drink, he will provide water."[103] The same logic applied to food. The *firqat* lived in the moment, and unless they were instructed not to eat their rations immediately, the food was consumed upon issuing.[104] If helicopters did not resupply the mission, the *firqat* would lose interest in the mission, or the BATT and SAF unit had to share their rations.[105] The *firqatmen* had intimate knowledge of the terrain from having spent most of their childhood herding cattle. The *firqatmen* knew the locations of water seepages and when they seasonally flowed. The *firqat* could cache extra ammunition ahead of missions.[106] As a consequence of these actions, the *firqat* could move extremely fast while scouting for SAF mission, often leaving the SAF unit unsupported.

Several BATT advisors also reiterated that the problems were not merely one-way. In fact, some of the BATT advisors that served multiple rotations with the *firqat* never developed trust of the SAF units. One Firqat Force officer acknowledged that after the first few missions with SAF nearly resulted in friendly-fire situations, he stopped informing the SAF about future missions. The officer quickly figured out that if the SAF knew that if the *firqat* had an interest in a particular area, then the SAF would try to conduct a mission at the location first.[107] British advisors in the SAF's Firqat Force also continued to have this view of the SAF after the BATT mission ended in 1973.[108]

The SAF eventually developed recommendation to use to the *firqats* as guide or reconnaissance force for their operations. The SAF understood that a *firqatman* could distinguish a Dhofari quicker than an Omani, Baluchi, or British Soldier. SAF commanders even consulted some *firqatmen* on enemy tactics and courses of action.[109] Following the first mission between the SAF and the Firqat Al Nasr, the SAF commander Lieutenant Colonel Fergus Mackain-Bremmer made a point to seek Jeapes out and compliment him on the performance of the *firqat*.[110]

By the end of the first year, the *firqats'* missions had quickly changed over the course of the first year from independent operations to operations in support of the SAF. The Firqat Salahdin's operations in Sudh and the Eagle's Nest soon became the exception to the rule. By 1974, the *firqats* were an established fact in Dhofar, the SAF's Firqat Force had assumed the partnership mission from the BATT, and the Commander, Dhofar had military control over the *firqats*.[111] Eventually the SAF and the *firqats* developed a systematic method to clear and hold the *jebel*.[112] These operations incorporated all five of the *Operation Storm's* fronts, used civil considerations in support of military operations, and employed food control operations in the form of water control. Most importantly, the operations reinforced the local tribal hierarchies. If the insurgency gained influence over a water well, the government forces capped it and the tribe moved to a new location.

Firqats after the Insurgency

In January 1972, the CSAF knew that he needed to have a discussion with the Sultan and the SAF about the long-term existence and employment of the *firqat*. Graham knew that Sultan supported the *firqat* model. He recommended the *firqat* eventually take over the pacification and home guard duties for the *jebel*. The BATT mission could not last forever, so another means of legitimizing the force was necessary.

Graham's recommendation recognized the legitimacy of the force and their contribution to fighting against the insurgency. The CSAF also acknowledged the importance of the BATT advisors to the *firqat* training and employment operations.[113] After the BATT left Oman, the SAF created the Firqat Force, an organization that resembled the BATT in structure and experience.

The *firqat* with their Firqat Force advisors continued to provide assistance to the SAF until the end of the insurgency. The *firqat*'s success during the insurgency ensured their survival after the conflict as a local security force. Although Qaboos declared the insurgency defeated on 4 December 1975, he appreciated the *firqatmen's* contribution to defeating the insurgency.[114] He took Graham's suggestions and employed them as a home guard. The *firqat* still provide security on the *jebel* today. Qaboos continues to employ the *firqat* for security in Dhofar. In 1990, the government paid each *firqatman* about 120-140 Omani riyals monthly ($370-$430).[115] The money also subsidizes the tribal way of life on the *jebel*.

Conclusion

Since the Dhofar insurgency is one of the few examples of a counterinsurgency campaign executed successfully, it is tempting to cherry-pick lessons from the campaign without considering its context. It is important to note that the odds heavily favored Sultan Qaboos once he started his program of social and economic reforms. The future counterinsurgent should consider a few other factors to prevent the application of a cookie-cutter Dhofar-like solution to future campaigns.

First, the Dhofar insurgency was a relatively small and isolated event. John Watts's five-front plan, *Operation Storm*, remained the overarching campaign plan for the entire war. Every commander remained committed to the five-front plan despite the fact that the BATT commander changed every four months, the SAF commanders changed every 18-24 months, and the CSAF changed every few years. Jeapes actually believed that this was the most important lesson of the war.[116]

Second, several veterans of the conflict acknowledge that the lack of media in the country allowed them to prosecute the campaign without external influences from Great Britain.[117] Most of the public back in Great Britain did not know the location of Dhofar, let alone that 22 SAS had deployed there in September 1970 to support the Sultan's program. In fact, the CSAF did not publish media guidance to the SAF regarding the presence of the SAS in Dhofar until 8 February 1972.[118] The public remained disengaged from the war because of the relatively small number of British casualties (BATT or SAF) during operations from 1970-1976. Furthermore, the events in Northern Ireland started to overshadow even rumors of SAS presence in Dhofar.[119] It is doubtful in the modern media age, with near-time reporting, that an interventionist power could achieve the same level of secrecy.

Third, the communist movement, PFLOAG, failed to address the tribes' grievances, and in the process the communists attempted to change the tribes against their will. PFLOAG attempted to break down the tribal structures. They encouraged, sometimes by force, the integration of men from different tribes into the same fighting units. Additionally, the Chinese and PDRY advisors to the *adoo* sought to reduce the influence of Islam on the *jebel* without understanding how deeply rooted Islam was to tribal culture.

Conversely, the BATT used the *firqat*s to reinforce the tribal structure. Several commanders, including Jeapes, credited the creation and employment of the *firqats* as a turning point in the insurgency.[120] The *firqatmen* supplemented the SAF during large operations, providing scouting, guiding, and other small unit operations. These duties allowed them to remain outside of the traditional military structure epitomized by the SAF.

The BATT encouraged the *firqat* to celebrate their Muslim traditions. The BATT allowed the *firqat* named their units after important Muslim warriors and Islamic holidays. The communists did not realize their mistake until late 1974, too late for the insurgency to recover from its military setbacks.[121] Both BATT and SAF veterans confirmed that they never attempted or were ordered to impose western, liberal democratic values on the Sultan or the Dhofaris.[122] In other words, the role of religion in society, the rights of women, and elections did not factor into the plan. Even after the so-called Arab Spring, Sultan Qaboos remains the head of one of the longest reigning authoritarian governments in the Middle East.

Fourth, Sultan Qaboos benefitted from a certain element of luck. Funding the counterinsurgency routinely used between one-third and half of the annual revenue of the Sultanate. This expenditure rate was unsustainable.[123] The British government assisted the Sultan slightly by subsidizing the cost of contract and seconded SAF officers. However, the Yom Kippur War in October 1973 drove up the price of crude oil over 70-percent.[124] Although government expenditure on the counterinsurgency programs remained high throughout the end of the war, the price increase on Oman's sole export allowed the Sultan to continue his reforms at an increased pace.

Finally, the SAS, operating as the BATT, had Soldiers uniquely qualified for working with irregular, local forces. Unlike British India, the SAS Soldiers were not picked specifically chosen to work with indigenous forces, although they had plenty of experience in that line of work before arriving in Dhofar. Before Dhofar, the SAS had worked with the Senoi Praak during the Malaya Emergency and the Border Scouts in Borneo against Indonesian incursions. Jeapes stated it takes a special type of Soldier to work with irregular forces because irregulars lack the discipline and work ethic of a regular Soldier.[125] The BATT veterans named many of the same characteristics that led Lawrence to appoint Lumsden the first commander of the Guides; patience, initiative, experience, and physical fitness. In the case of Dhofar, the SAS Soldiers were screened and selected for similar characteristics during their SAS selection and qualification. Even with centralized selection for the SAS, commanders still determined which SAS Soldiers were best suited to partner with the firqats when they rotated into the country.[126]

Additionally, the BATT took advantage of each advisor's individual experience, initiative, and leadership skills that SAS Soldiers are screened for during selection. The BATT advisors received broad guidance on the training and employment of their *firqat*. The tribal nature of the *firqat* meant that each set of advisors could not follow the same set of rules. What worked one set of advisors, would not work for another group. Mission command in this type of environment is necessary to produce a successful outcome. When the BATT left in September 1976, the SAF inherited a working system based on how the BATT visualized and assessed training, partnership, and mentoring.

If a future counterinsurgent remembers the context of the insurgency, then the Dhofar Insurgency provides another example of the successful recruitment, training, partnership, and employment of local irregular security forces. Just like the PIF, the *firqats* eventually joined the Sultan's regular security forces. In terms of size and scope of the mission, the BATT model in Dhofar is probably more representative of what an interventionist power could accomplish with an advisory force in the current political and media environment.

Notes

1.   The exact English translation of *firqat* is not clear. The Arabic word loosely translates to "task force" or "company" in military terms; however, other translations suggest it may only mean "group."

2.   Interview CF20110917DV0002_SESSION1A, 17 September 2011.

3.   The division of labor between the *firqat* and the SAF is an example of the mobile and static forces relationship described by Galula in his book. David Galula, *Counterinsurgency Warfare: Theory and Practice* (Westport, CT: Praeger Security International, 1964), 75-80; Ian Gardiner, *In the Service of the Sultan* (Yorkshire: Pen and Sword Books, 2007), 24.

4.   The *firqats* still exist and provide security in Dhofar.

5.   In 1798, the Sultanate did not include all of present-day Oman (including Dhofar). The Sultan of Muscat signed the initial treaty with British East Indian Company, who acted as an agent for the government.

6.   "Annex B to SD/29 39, History" Deane-Drummond Collection, LHCMA.

7.   The Wahabi and Saudi threat to the Sultanate continued until the 1950s. The Saudis contend that the Burami Oasis is part of their historical territory. The land disputes escalated as oil was discovered in the region. "Annex B to SD/29 39, History".

8.   J. E. Peterson, *Oman's Insurgencies: The Sultanate's Struggle for Supremacy* (London: SAQI, 2007), 40-41; "Annex B to SD/29 39, History," Deane-Drummond Collection, LHCMA.

9.   The 1913 succession crisis was the greatest threat to the Sultan's rule until the coup in 1970. The secular Sultan and the religious Imam informally shared power in Oman and Muscat. Occasionally, the Sultan and the Imam used events to rally support for uniting the Oman and Muscat under a single leader. In 1913, the newly elected Imam Salim bin Rashid al-Kharusi sought to consolidate control of Oman and Muscat under his authority. The Imam's tribes gradually took control of most of the country. The Indian Army rushed a regiment to Muscat at the start of the emergency, the 2d Queen Victoria's Own Rajput Light Infantry. The 102d King Edward's Own Grenadiers and the 95th Russell's Infantry later reinforced them. The two forces maneuvered against each other for more than a year before the Battle of Bayt al-Falaj. At the battle the Imam's tribesman attempted to overrun a series of sangers defended by the Indian troops resulting in nearly 500 casualties. The two sides did not engage in another battle during the crisis. Negotiations between the Sultan and the Imam went on for nearly five years. An agreement was reached after a tribesman assassinated the Imam. For a detailed account of the battle, see Peterson, 35-36, 41-46 and the 102d Grenadiers' regimental history.

10. The creation of the Sultan's army started following a visit by the Viceroy of India, Lord Hardinge, in February 1915 following the Battle of Bayt al-Falaj. During the visit he told the Sultan that he could not depend on the presence of Indian troops forever. Major L.B.H. Haworth forwarded a proposal to governments in Muscat and Delhi for creation a regiment using 200-300 Baluchi levies. This regiment was known as the Muscat Levy Corps (later the Muscat Regiment) and was formed in April 1921. Peterson, 47-49.

11. Sultan Said gradually replaced the Royal Air Force squadron with his own planes, a process accelerated by the signing of new military agreement on 28 July 1958. The Sultan continued to use British contract and seconded pilots to fly the planes. The air force is formally known as the Sultan of Oman's Air Force, or SOAF. "The Exchange of Letters between the Government of the United Kingdom of Great Britain and Northern Ireland and the Sultan of Muscat and Oman concerning the Sultan's Armed Forces, Civil Aviation, Royal Air Force facilities and Economic Development in Muscat and Oman, London 25 July 1958" HMSO Cmnd. 507, Treaty Series No. 28 (London: HMSO, 1958).

12. Calvin Allen, Jr. and W. Lynn Rigsbee, II, *Oman Under Qaboos: From Coup to Constitution, 1970-1996* (London: Frank Cass, 2000), 12-15.

13. This insurgency is described in greater detail later in the chapter. Frank Kitson helped plan the British intervention. He used the insurgency as a case study in *Bunch of Five*. See *Bunch of Five* Chapter 3 for a detailed account of the British response.

14. Walter C. Ladwig III, "Supporting allies in counterinsurgency: Britain and the Dhofar Rebellion," *Small Wars and Insurgencies* 19, no. 1 (2008): 71.

15. For comparison, Dhofar is approximately the same size as Wales. Alexander Melamid, "Dhofar," *Geographical Review* 74, no. 1 (January 1984): 106.

16. Tony Jeapes, *SAS Secret War: Operation Storm in the Middle East* (Mechanicsburg: Stackpole Books, 1996), 20.

17. Melamid, 106.

18. Population numbers for Dhofar differ greatly based on the source because no accurate census was taken on the jebel until after the war concluded. Beckett cites the lower number for 1970, while Meland cites the higher number for 1977. In reality, the population is probably closer to Meland's number since it unlikely the population doubled in a seven-year span, and Meland's number is close to the post-war census number of 70,000. Interview with Civil Aid Development worker, 14 February 2011; Ian F.W. Beckett "The Counterinsurgency Campaign in Dhofar, 1965-75," in *Counterinsurgency in the Modern Warfare*, ed. Daniel Marston and Carter Malkasian (Long Island City: Osprey, 2010), 175; Melamid, 106.

19. Peter Thwaites, *Arabian Command* (unpublished) Thwaites Collection, Box 1/1, LHCMA, 70.

20. Jeapes, 19.

21. A former BATT solder and civil servant in Dhofar also reinforced this point with several examples. Interview CF20110914DV0001_SESSION1A, 14 September 2011; Peter Thwaites, *Arabian Command,* Thwaites Collection 1/1, LHCMA, 29.

22. Beckett in Marston, 175

23. Peterson, 186.

24. The only other province to share this "special" status was Muscat. Allen and Rigsbee, 7.

25. Peterson, 186.

26. Allen and Rigsbee, 2.

27. Allen and Rigsbee.

28. Although educated at Mayo College, "the Eton of India", Sultan Said bin Taimur once remarked to his army commander-in-chief, David Smiley, a British officer seconded to the SAF, that better health care and education resulted in the British loss of India. David Smiley, *Arabian Assignment* (London: Cooper, 1975), 41.

29. Allen and Rigsbee, 11.

30. This fact is probably an exaggeration, but it does illustrate the primitive nature of the infrastructure and Said's resistance to modernity prior to the first insurgency. Other sources suggest that there were three paved roads in Muscat prior to the 1958 rebellion, and Said even tried to introduce a state-run taxi service early in his rule. Roger Cole and Richard Belfield, *SAS Operation Storm: Nine Men Against Four Hundred in Britain's Secret War* (London: Hodder and Stoughton Ltd., 2011), 39-40; Allen and Rigsbee, 10.

31. Allen and Rigsbee, 11.

32. Beckett in Marston, 176.

33. J. H. McKeown, "Britain and Oman: The Dhofar War and its Significance" (M.Phil thesis, University of Cambridge, 1981), 34.

34. Corran Purdon, *List the Bugle: Reminiscences of an Irish Soldier* (Antrim: Greystone Books, Ltd., 1993), 244.

35. Cole and Belfield, 40.

36. The Trucial Oman Scouts contained one squadron (X Squadron) comprised of Dhofari tribesman. Seconded British officers led the military unit. Interestingly, the organization was multi-tribal. Interview CF20110917DV0002_SESSION1A, 17 September 2011.

37. Interview CF20110914DV0001_SESSION1A, 14 September 2011; Jeapes, 25; Paul Sibley, *A Monk in the SAS* (London: Spiderwize, 2011), 62.

38. A small region Baluchistan was under Sultan of Oman's control until 1958. The Sultan retained the right to recruit Baluchi males for service in Oman as part of the treaty returning the port city of Gwadur to Pakistan in 1958. The Sultan recruited males for the SAF and police heavily from this area until 1979 because they tended to be more professional than local males. Additionally, these forces tended to work for less than money than Omanis. David C. Arkless, *The Secret War* (London: William Limbar, 1988), 25; John Akehurst, *We Won a War* (Guildford: Briddles Limited, 1982), 34.

39. Thwaites, 82.

40. The Sultan authorized Captain St. John Armitage to form the Dhofar Force in 1955. The force was never representative of the Dhofaris. The approximately 60 Soldiers were initially Baluch, although they were gradually replaced with Dhofari tribesman and slaves. The unit manned a number of smaller garrisons including the Sultan's Palace. The first three commanders of the Dhofar Force were British-seconded officers, including a former CO of the Trucial Oman Scouts. Eventually, command of the unit went a contracted Pakistani officer. After the assassination attempt in 1966, the unit was ineffective due to decreased resources allocated to it. Sultan Qaboos disbanded the unit after the coup in 1970. Peterson, 187-188.

41. The assassination attempt also resulted in the Sultan's self-exile to his palace in Salalah. Peterson, 202-203.

42. P. S. Allfree was a British officer seconded to the Muscat Regiment. He later served as the Sultan's chief intelligence officer. During an inspection of the prisons in Muscat he described the prisoners as confined to the same position day after day. Eventually, the prisoner's joints calcified, which resulted in permanent state of excruciating pain. Almost ironically, the Sultan believed that the death penalty was contrary to the Islamic faith. P. S. Allfree, *Warlords of Oman* (London: Robert Hale, 2008), 162-164; John Townsend, *Oman: Making of a Modern State* (London: C. Helm, 1977), 11.

43. Saudi Arabia used Ghalid and his followers as a proxy force to pursue its claim to the Burami Oasis. Peterson, 77-78.

44. This campaign is also referred to as the Northern Insurgency and the Jebel Akhdar Insurgency.

45. "Annex B to SD/29 39, History," Deane-Drummond Collection, LHCMA.

46. Peterson, 83-84.

47. "Annex B to SD/29 39, History," Deane-Drummond Collection, LHCMA.

48. Jeapes, 18.

49. McKeown, 21.

50. Initially, the SAF did not have forces stationed in Dhofar because the Sultan remained concerned with the tribes that rebelled in the north in 1957-1959. The Dhofar Force lacked the manpower to pursue the rebels following attacks. Peterson, 189-191.

51. Later in the war, these countries met annually to determine the methods and conditions of continuing to support the insurgency. Support included money, weapons, vehicles, and sanctuary. Eventually, Egypt and Saudi Arabia discontinued support for the insurgency because of ideological differences and in an attempt to normalize relations with the United Kingdom. "People's Front for the Liberation of Oman" (4 November 1974), Graham Collection 2/1, MEC, St. Antony's College, Oxford, 1-2; Peterson, 196.

52. Thwaites, *Arabian Command*, 10-11; Allen and Rigsbee, 27; Peterson, 200-212.

53. Ranulph Fiennes, *Living Dangerously* (London: Athenaeum, 1988), 150.

54. Jonathan Walker, "Red Wolves and British Lions: The Conflict in Aden," in *Counterinsurgency in the Modern Warfare*, ed. Daniel Marston and Carter Malkasian (Long Island City: Osprey, 2010), 135.

55. Peter Calvocoressi, *World Politics Since 1945*, 9th ed. (Harlow: Pearson Education Limited, 2009), 410-412.

56. In 1964, the 1st Battalion, Irish Guards attacked Hauf from Aden in support of Muscat Regiment attack on the Dhofar side of the border. The Guards arrested nearly 50 wanted men, vetted them, and turned them over to the SAF for transport to Muscat. Thwaites, *Arabian Command*, 31.

57. China provided arms, ammunition, and military advisors to PFLOAG. They trained 30 Dhofaris as military leaders and political commissars at the anti-imperialist school in Peking. One Chinese advisor was actually killed in Dhofar still wearing his uniform. Thwaites, 117, 119.

58. Jeapes, 26-27.

59. The Midway Road served as the dividing line between the east and west regions. Salalah and the surrounding are was the third region. Allen and Rigsbee, 28.

60. Arabic for "enemy."

61. Sibley, 68; Allen and Rigsbee, 66.

62. The SAF assessment cited eight primary problems for the failure of the Sultan's counterinsurgency campaign. The SAF assessment is based on lessons learned and codified by contemporary theorists of the period including Sir Robert Thompson, Frank Kitson, and David Galula. The problems included: (1) No police or Special Branch; (2) No resettlement of the population; (3) Scant food control; (4) No surrender or amnesty terms; (5) No psyops or propaganda; (6) No hearts and minds; (7) No

civil government on the *jebel*; (8) Comparatively little intelligence. SAF Report, "Dhofar Operations as of January 1970" Thwaites Collection, Box 1/2, LHCMA.

63. Gardiner, 24.

64. Allen and Rigsbee, 28-29; Jeapes, 28.

65. Peterson, 243.

66. Allen and Rigsbee, 67; Jeapes, 29-30.

67. John Watts, "An Outline Plan to Restore the Situation in Dhofar Using Special Air Service Regiment Troops" (6 April 1970), Graham Collection 2/2, MEC, St. Antony's College, Oxford. It is curious to note that Watts's assessment took place prior to the coup. Although the British government has never admitted to assisting with the 23 July 1970 palace coup, there is a lot of evidence to suggest that they knew it would take place in the near-term including the prepositioning of the aircraft that carried Sultan Said out of Dhofar.

68. Headquarters, Sultan's Armed Forces, "Plans 7" (20 November 1970), Graham Collection 2/2, MEC, St. Antony's College, Oxford.

69. The British citizenry largely remained ignorant of the BATT's presence in Dhofar following the defeat in Aden. The deployment of troops also violated Whitehall's disengagement criteria from interest east of the Suez Canal. Casualties could draw unnecessary attention to the mission and force the BATT withdrawal. Jeapes, 32-33, 63.

70. Interview CF20110914DV0001_SESSION1A, 14 September 2011

71. Jeapes, 40.

72. No one is sure who suggested forming the firqats from surrendered enemy personnel first, Jeapes or Mubarak. Neither Graham nor Watts included in their guidance for execution. The use of former enemies is not without precedent. Kitson formed the pseudo-gangs during the Mau-Mau Uprising in 1952-1956 in Kenya from turned insurgents. See Kitson's, *Bunch of Five*, Part I, Chapter 3 for more information on the creation of the pseudo-gangs. Additionally, Lumsden's initial recruitment of natives for the Guides included Sikhs that had fought against the British only two years before in the First Sikh War. He also included tribesman that were wanted criminals. General Sir Peter S. Lumsden and George R. Elsmie, *Lumsden of the Guides: A Sketch of the Life of Lieut.-Gen. Sir Harry Burnett Lumsden, K.C.S.I., C.B., with Selections from his Correspondence and Occasional Papers* (London: John Murray, 1900), 35, 66-67. Interestingly, none of the BATT Soldiers' memoirs, including Jeapes's, mentioned these organizations as an influence for the *firqat*.

73. Ibid, 50.

74. Headquarters, Sultan's Armed Forces, "Plans 7" (12 February 1971), Graham Collection 2/2, MEC, St. Antony's College, Oxford.

75. Sibley, 62.

76. Interview CF20110912J0001_SESSION1A, 12 September 2011.

77. "Irregular Forces – SAF View" Graham Collection, MEC, St. Antony's College, Oxford.

78. R.C. Nightingale, "The Future of Dhofar" (15 July 1972) Graham Collection, MEC, St. Antony's College, Oxford.

79. The Bait Kathir consists of two factions, one north occupying the *negd*, and the other south residing in the coastal plain west of Salalah. The BATT referred to the southern faction as the al-Kathir. The Bait Kathir consisted of more than a dozen sub-tribes. "Summary of Precedents: Anti-Guerrilla Operations" (July 1971) Graham Collection 2/1, MEC, St. Antony's College, Oxford; Jeapes, 54.

80. Jeapes, 57.

81. After the SAS agreed to train the Bait Kathir's Firqat Al Nasr, several other tribal leaders approached the BATT requesting permission to form tribal *firqat*s. The Firqat A'asifat (Eastern Mahra), Firqat Tariq Bin Zeead (Western Mahra), and Firqat Khalid Bin Waalid (Bait Ma'asheni) followed the Firqat Al Nasr model for SAS mentorship, training, and employment. In early 1972, eleven *firqat*s existed with 25 to 140 Soldiers in each unit. "Irregular Forces – SAF View" Graham Collection, MEC, St. Antony's College, Oxford. When BATT operations in Dhofar ceased in 1974, the eleven tribal *firqat*s contained nearly 2,000 SEPs. Jeapes, 213.

82. Tactics instruction included interdiction of enemy supply routes, ambushes, raids, working with SAF operations, and leading tribes against enemy hardcore elements. "Irregular Forces – SAF View" Graham Collection 2/2, MEC, St. Antony's College, Oxford.

83. Interview CF20110912J0001_SESSION1A, 12 September 2011; Interview CF20110913C0001_SESSION1A, 13 September 2011.

84. "Irregular Forces – SAF View" Graham Collection 2/2, MEC, St. Antony's College, Oxford.

85. Interview CF20110914DV0001_SESSION1A, 14 September 2011; Interview ICF20110914MS0001_ SESSION1A, 14 September 2011.

86. "BATT Notes on the Raising and Training of Irregular Forces in Dhofar" Graham Collection 2/2, MEC, St. Antony's College, Oxford.

87. The *firqatmen* preferred the AK-47 to the FN rifle, the SAF service rifle, because it could fire on automatic. When a SEP came in to join a *firqat,* he surrendered his communist issued AK-47 in return for the weapon bounty and was issued a FN. The BATT demonstrated during each training period that the FN was a superior fire in terms of long-range marksmanship, an exercise that the *firqatmen* viewed with skepticism. Interview CF20110912J0001_SESSION1A, 12 September 2011.

88. Interview CF20110914MS0001_SESSION1A, 14 September 2011.

89. A former BATT commander remarked that one of the first actions by a tribe when welcoming a new SEP was to pray with the individual. Most SEPs wanted to regain a sense of community after leaving the communist lines. Allowing the SEP to pray to with his tribe reinforced both the tribal lines and tenets of Islam that the communists sought to destroy on the *jebel*. Interview CF20110912J0001_SESSION1A, 12 September 2011.

90. The four-man element usually consisted of a team commander (usually a noncommissioned officer), an Arab linguist, a medic, and a weapons specialist. Additionally, one member of each team had a signal (communications) specialty. Interview CF20110914MS0001_SESSION1A, 14 September 2011. The BATT model of four-man teams intentionally differed from the US model of partnership with the highland Montagnard tribes in Vietnam. During initial operations trust between the trainers and the security force was not established. As a result, the trainers maintained a guard to ensure the security force did not attempt to kill them in their sleep. Four-Soldier elements allowed for two Soldiers to maintain awareness of the security force, operate the radio, and keep each other awake, while the other team of two Soldiers slept. British observers in Vietnam noted that American advisors were often sleep deprived due to the two-Soldier advisor structure. Interview CF20110917DV0002_ SESSION1A, 17 September 2011.

91. Interview CF20110914DV0001_SESSION1A, 14 September 2011; Sibley, 93.

92. Interview CF20110914DV0001_SESSION1A, 14 September 2011; Interview CF20110917DV0002_SESSION1A, 17 September 2011; Gardiner, 159.

93. Interview CF20110917DV0002_SESSION1A, 17 September 2011.

94. Interview CF20110912J0001_SESSION1A, 12 September 2011.

95. Interview CF20110912J0001_SESSION1A, 12 September 2011; Interview CF20110913C0001_SESSION1A, 13 September 2011; Interview CF20110914DV0001_ SESSION1A 14 September 2011; Interview CF20110917DV0002_SESSION1A, 17 September 2011.

96. Jeapes, 65.

97. Jeapes, 76-81.

98. Interview CF20110912J0001_SESSION1A, 12 September 2011; Interview CF20110913C0001_SESSION1A, 13 September 2011; Interview CF20110914DV0001_ SESSION1A 14 September 2011: Interview CF20110917DV0002_SESSION1A, 17 September 2011.

99. Sultan Qaboos suspended the practice and enforcement of blood feuds immediately following the coup. The practice still continued with the *jebeli* tribes, but at a much-diminished rate. Interview CF20110912J0001_SESSION1A, 12 September 2011.

100. Headquarters, Dhofar, "INT/15/D Firqa Salahdin – Discipline," Graham Collection 2/2, MEC, St. Antony's College, Oxford.

101. Jeapes, 114.

102. Gardiner, 157.

103. Interview CF20110914DV0001_SESSION1A, 14 September 2011.

104. "BATT Notes on the Raising and Training of Irregular Forces in Dhofar," Graham Collection, MEC, St. Antony's College, Oxford.

105. Paul Sibley suggested that the *firqat* took their rations and actually gave them to their families as a means of support. Sibley, 92.

106. Interview CF20110914DV0001_SESSION1A, 14 September 2011.

107. CF20110914DV0001_SESSION1A.

108. After the BATT mission ended, the Sultan, with advise from the CSAF, created a new organization, the Firqat Force, to take over the BATT's training and partnership mission. Firqat Force advisors typically had served at least one rotation with the SAF or the BATT previously and volunteered to work with the *firqat*. Although the Firqat Force was supposed to look like BATT's four-Soldier teams, each *firqat* typically had only advisor. At one point in 1973, one advisor had responsibility for three different tribal firqats. The tribes correctly pointed out that the advisor could not represent the interests of all three tribes to the government, and his creditability with the tribes suffered from the cultural oversight. Interview CF20110917DV0002_SESSION1A, 17 September 2011.

109. "Irregular Forces – SAF View," Graham Collection, MEC, St. Antony's College, Oxford.

110. Jeapes, 110-111.

111. Gardiner, 159.

112. Colonel John Akehurst, the Dhofar Brigade Commander in 1974-75 outlined a typical operation: 1. A SAF operation in strength supported by a *firqat* secures a position of the *firqat*'s choice, which dominated its tribal area; 2. Military engineers build a track to the position giving road access, followed by an airstrip if possible; 3. A drill is brought down the track (to bore a well for the local civilians) followed by a Civil Action Team (who set up a) shop, school, clinic, and mosque; 4. SAF thins out to the minimum security; 5. Water is pumped to the surface and into distribution systems prepared by military engineers to offer storage points for humans, and troughs for animals; 6. Civilians come in from miles around and talk to the *firqat*, SAF, and Government representatives. They are told that enemy activity in the area will result in the water being cut off; 7. Civilians move out to the surrounding areas and tell the enemy not to interfere with what is obviously 'a good thing.'; 8. Enemy, very dependent on civilians, stops all aggressive action and either goes elsewhere or hides; 9. Tribal area is secure; 10. All SAF are withdrawn. Almost all of the operations followed the same pattern. Akehurst, 63-64.

113. "CSAF Memorandum" (9 January 1972), Graham Collection, MEC, St. Antony's College, Oxford.

114. Akehurst, 173.

115. Jorg Janzen, "The Destruction of Resources among the Mountain Nomads of Dhofar" in *The Transformation of Nomadic Society in the Arab East.* ed., Martha Mundy and Basim Musallam (Cambridge: Cambridge University Press, 2000), 168.

116. Jeapes, 234.

117. Interview CF20110914DV0001_SESSION1A, 14 September 2011; Interview CF20110917DV0002_SESSION1A, 17 September 2011.

118. Headquarters, Sultan's Armed Forces, "Plans/7: References to Presence in Dhofar of SAS Personnel" (8 February 1972), Graham Collection 2/2, MEC, St. Antony's College, Oxford.

119. Interview CF20110913C0001_SESSION1A, 13 September 2011.

120. Jeapes, 236-237.

121. Interview CF20110917DV0002_SESSION1A, 17 September 2011.

122. Interview CF20110917DV0002_SESSION2A, 17 September 2011.

123. D. L. Price, "Oman: Insurgency and Development" (London: Institute for the Study of Conflict, 1975), 13.

124. Daniel Yergin, *The Prize: The Epic Quest for Oil, Money, and Power* (New York: Simon and Shuster, 2008), 587.

125. Jeapes, 236.

126. Interview CF20110917DV0002_SESSION1A, 14 September 2011.

Chapter 5

Iraq And Beyond

I don't know if you are one of those people who pretend to despise history. As a matter of fact if you do, you're a fraud. You exist on history like everyone else. Frontier and Afghan operations have been very fully written up. If you read the books you'll find the same mistakes made with monotonous regularity.

- Colonel J. P. Villiers-Stuart, *Letters of a Once Punjab Frontier Force Officer*

The campaigns in Iraq and Afghanistan continue to demonstrate the importance of building local irregular security forces to fighting an insurgency. In both campaigns the counterinsurgent has attempted to build local irregular security forces without the host nation's commitment to the solution. Nevertheless, partnership between the counterinsurgent and the local irregular security force is one the most important factors to determining whether an indigenous security force is successful in fighting an insurgency. Partnership between the security force and advisors can increase the security force legitimacy by combining the irregular Soldiers' knowledge of the local conditions with the advisor's knowledge of organization, tactics, and resources. This partnership can professionalize the irregular force over time and enhance their legitimacy in the eyes of the indigenous government and the population. Simultaneously, the indigenous host government needs to be involved in the process of creating the security force to help ensure its legitimacy within the security apparatus and with the population. By having both the government and the military involved in building local irregular security forces, the counterinsurgent can seek to restore balance between the three sides of Clausewitz's paradoxical trinity.

A case-study analysis of this problem has significant limitations for future counterinsurgents. First and foremost, no two counterinsurgencies are exactly identical. The local conditions are extremely important for determining how the campaign is prosecuted, especially for the interventionist power. Past experience is not a predictor of future success. The application of the Iraq surge's "winning strategy" to Afghanistan in 2009 has not produced the same results. Enemy attacks have not dropped by 60-percent, the Afghans have not overtly rejected the Taliban, and the populace has not spontaneously attempted to create a local security solution, despite the introduction of 30,000 additional coalition troops.[1]

The Dhofar campaign also demonstrated that counterinsurgency lessons from other campaigns do not necessarily transfer to the conditions of other conflicts. The Sultan's Armed Forces assessment of the counterinsurgency effort in January 1970 listed eight shortcomings with their strategy.[2] The shortcomings listed showed the influence of previous counterinsurgency operations in Malaya, Kenya, and Borneo. Although the SAF believed that these shortcomings were important to the campaign, only two significantly influenced the resulting campaign, the lack of an information campaign to inform the population and the lack of campaign to improve local living conditions for the Dhofaris. The counterinsurgents never corrected the first shortcoming, the lack of police or Special Branch forces. Instead the *firqat* acted as a pseudo-Special Branch, gathered intelligence, and reinforced the tribal-based government on the *jebel*.

The local conditions of two different counterinsurgencies will probably never be the same; however, as Colonel Villiers-Stuart suggested in his *Letters* there are some lessons for the counterinsurgent within the case studies that applied to both campaigns. The local security force needs to have legitimacy in the eyes of the state and the populace. The local irregular force should reflect the local conditions. The government's involvement in building the security force and addressing the local grievance is important to its future success. Finally, not all Soldiers will make good advisors.

Legitimacy

The local irregular security force must have legitimacy in eyes of the state and the people on the ground. The government needs to believe that the local irregular force is ultimately answerable to the government, not the advisory force. The British made this mistake with the Khyber Rifles, and it ultimately contributed to their disbandment in 1919. Colonel Robert Warburton served as the Political Officer, Khyber when the Khyber Rifles were formed in 1878. He worked daily with the irregular force and its native commander, Mohammad Aslam, until they both retired in 1897. Shortly thereafter during the start of the 1897 Frontier Uprising, the Soldiers deserted their positions, surrendered control of the pass, and lost 118 men in the process. The Soldiers did not trust their new commander, and the native officer lacked the standing with his men in a crisis. Their actions revealed that the Soldiers were loyal to the commander and advisor, not necessarily the government. In 1919, the British disbanded the unit and moved more trustworthy troops to the pass before the Rifles' loyalty to the government could be tested.[3]

An interventionist power building local security forces without consent of the internationally recognized government could face similar problems with legitimacy. In this case the interventionist power is potentially violating the Westphalian system of sovereignty. The Westphalian system has three primary tenets, the sovereignty of states and their fundamental right to political self-determination, legal equality between states without regard to size, population, or influence, and the principle of non-intervention of one state in the internal affairs of another state.[4] An interventionist force must work through, not around, the national government to avoid violating these tenets. Otherwise, the government and the local populace could view the security force as a different form of threat.[5] This situation is one of the problems with President Karzai's reluctance to build the Afghan Local Police (ALP) program, which the government as complained is hard to control and potentially dangerous.[6]

The Sons of Iraq (SoI) program in Iraq could potentially fail after the US military withdraws at the end of 2011 because it lacks legitimacy in eyes of the Government of Iraq. The United States built this irregular force without consulting the Baghdad government. Several Shia leaders considered the Sunni militia a potential future threat. The SoI program grew quickly to 103,000 mostly Sunnis legally carrying weapons.[7] Furthermore, Multi-National Forces-Iraq did not control the development, numbers, or training of this force with a policy standardizing procedures. Instead, the headquarters delegated responsibility for the program to brigade commanders. As a result, most units, already adverse to partnership with national forces, took a hands-off approach with the Sons of Iraq. Some tribal leaders viewed Prime Minister Nouri Al-Malaki's maneuvers in 2007 to weaken the Awakening through a divide and rule policy. He offered jobs to SoI Soldiers in the Diyala Province, arrested former insurgents that assumed leadership roles in the Awakening, and initially refused to fund the local force.[8]

The fact that the Government of Iraq consistently failed to meet milestones for the SoI program despite assurances to the US government also suggests a legitimacy problem with the force. It failed to meet the mid-2009 deadline to integrate the nearly 76,000 Sons of Iraq into the government despite an agreement to do so with the Multi-National Forces-Iraq. In October 2008, only 8,748 SoIs had transferred into Iraqi Security Forces.[9] A second deadline at the beginning of January 2010 also passed with less than 54-percent compliance.[10] Similar deadlines regarding the Government of Iraq taking over the payment of the Sons of Iraq in

November 2008 also resulted in the US guaranteeing the payrolls to prevent the local security forces from walking off the job.

The Dhofar counterinsurgency is an example where the Sultan's Armed Forces and the local police lacked legitimacy in the eyes of the populace. The populace viewed the Omani police forces as interlopers due to the ethnic and cultural differences. The *firqat*s did not have the same problem, although they did encounter a different form of the problem. The tribes refused to cross into each other's territory to conduct missions. The tribal *firqats* had legitimacy within their tribal area, but their value decreased when operating in other tribal areas.[11]

Another method of gaining legitimacy through the use of a local irregular security is to fully integrate them within the counterinsurgent's "whole of government" approach. In British India, the PIF escorted the British political officers when they paid subsidies and leveled fines against the tribes. The PIF also made arrests when they were required. In Dhofar, the *firqat* secured provided security within their tribal areas while the Civil Aid Teams built roads, airstrips, and wells.[12] The *firqat* stayed in the area even after the SAF moved on to the next mission. The local irregular force can then become the face of the counterinsurgent and the government.

Reinforce the Local Systems

The counterinsurgent should build local security forces with the existing systems rather than trying to change society. In British India and Dhofar, the British trainers reinforced the existing tribal and class systems. The Sunni Awakening initially started with a tribal element in Al-Anbar Province.[13] During a counterinsurgency the army should not be a social experiment to build a national identity, gender equality, or other reforms. The indigenous national government should introduce these reforms.

Conversely, the initial BATT approach and the insurgents in Dhofar failed to create irregular forces that broke down the existing tribal system. The communist advisors to PFLOAG desired to break down both the tribal and Islamic elements of life on the *jebel*. The communist realized too late that they were alienating the local populace by violently suppressing these elements. Salim Mubarak and Major Tony Jeapes attempted to create a multi-tribal irregular unit, the Firqat Salahdin, on the belief that fighters could overcome traditional tribal rivalry. Although initially successful, the Firqat Salahdin only fought as a multi-tribal organization for five months.[14]

The use of the local populace in an irregular security force can give the counterinsurgent force an advantage. Sometimes the use of national forces is not the best solution to defeating an insurgency with a local grievance. This is a problem that is probably exacerbated in countries where the populace lacks a strong sense of national identity like Dhofar and the North-West Frontier's tribal areas. The local populace can also offer the counterinsurgent other advantages over the national forces. In British India, the British opted not to use national forces for a different reason. The Indian Army lacked the training and equipment to operate efficiently in the mountains. The Guides were able to capture the fort at Govindgarh during the Second Sikh War precisely because they looked and spoke like the local populace.[15]

Over time the local irregular security forces can be fully integrated into the regular forces. The PIF operated as a separate force for about thirty years before their integration into the Indian Army. The PIF served in the regular army, deploying to the Middle East and even Europe with the Indian Army. Dhofar is another example of integration even though the force continues to only provide security within their tribal areas. A sense of Dhofari and Omani identity is slowly emerging in the region. The *firqat* still patrol the *jebel* under the nominal command of the Sultan's Firqat Force.

The Peshmerga in Iraq is another local security forces that produced a slightly different outcome than the Sons of Iraq program. The Peshmerga is a tribally based Kurdish force in northern Iraq, southern Turkey, and northwest Iran. In this case, the Peshmerga eventually joined the national army. Entire Peshmerga battalions joined the Iraqi National Guard in 2004. Those battalions proved important for fighting the insurgency in Mosul after other non-tribal units refused to fight. The battalions are now part of Iraqi 2nd Division stationed in Mosul and part of the Iraqi Army Northern Forces.[16]

Selection of Advisors

Not every Soldier can effectively serve as an advisor. The officers and Soldiers directly involved in building local indigenous forces should be chosen based their ability and demonstration of certain traits. The most important trait is that the advisor has a desire to perform the job. Commanders in North-West Frontier and Dhofar chose trainers for their flexibility, tolerance, patience, physical fitness, and initiative. Advisory duty is a careful balancing act of respecting the irregular forces' culture and meeting the needs of the military. The BATT advisors in Dhofar cited the case of one of their own trainers that went "native", meaning he tried to replicate being a Dhofari to build trust. The *firqat* did not respect the Soldier, and the BATT did not feel that he could conduct his job objectively.[17]

The trainers and the local force should share risk when working together in order to build trust and confidence in each other. Theater policy in Iraq and Afghanistan prevented coalition troops from sharing quarters and supplies with indigenous forces, both regular and irregular. Although troops often share a common base, the two forces are segregated. Furthermore in Iraq, training teams could not work with indigenous forces without a platoon-sized force protection element. In some cases the number of Soldiers protecting the advisory team equaled the number of Iraqi Soldiers, which can undermine the government's message of who is control of the security mission. Casualties will occur with this system; however, the long-term benefits of close partnership should outweigh the risk. Since 2005, 52 "green-on-blue" attacks in Afghanistan resulted in coalition deaths. However, 36-percent of the attacks were attributed to combat-stress related incidents, whereas only 23-percent of the attacks resulted from Taliban infiltration of the organization.[18] In both PIF and *firqats*, the trainers rarely numbered more than ten in a battalion-sized element; however, in both cases there is not one instance of an irregular murdering an advisor.

The military needs to take steps to ensure that advisory duty a desirable job to volunteer for in the future. Political and military leaders should realize that good training teams as strategic assets similar to Special Forces. The military needs to take steps to ensure that officers and Soldiers recruited for training teams remain competitive for promotion and command within the larger army.[19] In 2009, Secretary of Defense Robert Gates wrote that it remained to be seen if the Pentagon could adapt the personnel and promotion systems to reward officers and Soldiers for taking advisor assignments.[20]

The two case studies primarily examined in this study are limited to primarily to the British experience. It does not suggest that the British have mastered the training of local irregular forces. In fact, the British failure to create Military Training Teams for even the national forces during *Operation Telic* in Iraq might suggest that the British have forgotten this past experience.[21]

An officer or Soldier's exposure to foreign cultures prior to assuming an advising mission is another area that should be examined in the future. Many of the advisors working in both British India and Dhofar either grew up or worked outside of the United Kingdom prior to serving in the advisor role. A former US division chief of staff and brigade commander also suggested that US Army units stationed in Germany performed better than US-based units early in Iraq. He attributed this observation to the number of rotations that Germany-based units conducted in the Balkans and Eastern Europe. In effect, these deployments exposed Soldiers to working with foreign Soldiers.[22]

Partnership with local irregular forces should remain an important aspect of any future counterinsurgency effort. Local forces help the government and the military maintain influence with populace during an insurgency. The advisory force can help legitimize an irregular force by offering it training, resources, and experience. Additionally, the advisory force can serve as a check to ensure accountability back to the government during military and civil operations.

Good advisors and advisory teams can be strategic assets. For this reason, advisors need to be carefully chosen for the job. Successful partnership missions rely on a small number of Soldiers having an effect on a large number of irregulars. In both the North-West Frontier and Dhofar, teams of as few as four Soldiers partnered with platoon and company-sized elements. Their partnership allowed the host indigenous government to relay their message to the people. The forces also reported back to the national government on what was occurring in areas that were not fully under government control. Advisory missions, when conducted well, can result in the irregular force's integration into the regular forces of the counterinsurgent. In a time when both the US and the UK are reducing the end strengths of their militaries, partnership has the potential to be a small investment, large pay-off military mission.

Notes

1. The Iraq surge of troops coincided with a 60-percent drop in attacks and a 70-percent drop in civilian deaths. Sunni tribal leaders rejected Al-Qaeda's continued violence in the country, and they declared support for the Government of Iraq. Sunni leaders formed the Concerned Local Citizens program, the Sons of Iraq, and other local security solutions to keep Al-Qaeda and other malcontents out of their neighborhoods. Kimberly Kagan, *The Surge: A Military History* (New York: Encounter Books, 2009), 196.

2. The eight shortcomings are listed in Chapter 4. SAF Report, "Dhofar Operations as of January 1970," Thwaites Collection, Box 1/2, LHCMA.

3. Trench, 8-11.

4. Hans J. Morgenthau, *Politics Among Nations: The Struggle for Power and Peace,* 7th ed. (New York: McGraw-Hill, 2006), 284.

5. Indian-administered Kashmir is an example of counterinsurgency where this is true. Paramilitary forces operate in Kashmir under the Armed Forces Special Powers Act. The populace views this force with contempt, often resulting to throwing stones at the militiamen to provoke a response. In 2010, India started to recruit local Kashmiri youth for the paramilitary forces in Jammu and Kashmir to change the face of the paramilitary forces in the hope of gaining local legitimacy. See Sumantra Rose's *Kashmir: Roots of Conflict, Paths to Peace* (Cambridge: Harvard University Press: 2005); Sumit Ganguly "Explaining the Kashmir Insurgency: Political Mobilization and Institutional Decay," *International Security* 21, no. 2 (Autumn, 1996): 76-107; Ashutosh Varshney, "India, Pakistan, and Kashmir: Antimonies of Nationalism," *Asian Survey* 31, no. 11 (November 1991): 997-1019 for more information on the role of paramilitary forces in the Kashmir insurgency.

6. Allissa J. Rubin and Richard A. Opeel, Jr., "US and Afghanistan Debate More Village Forces," *The New York Times,* 12 July 2010.

7. Thomas E. Ricks, *The Gamble: General Petraeus and the American Military Adventure in Iraq* (New York: Penguin Books, 2009), 203-204.

8. The arrests of Adel Mushadani in east Baghdad proved especially controversial within the SoI program, because it nearly confirmed the government's fears of an armed opposition. Malaki ordered Mushdani's arrest for crimes he committed as an insurgent prior to assuming the leadership of the Fadhil SoI unit. A day later, the military arrested Raad Ali, the SoI leader in the west Baghdad neighborhood of Ghazaliya. The SoI in that neighborhood threatened the government with violence if they held Mushadani. Ned Parker and Usama Redha, "Sons of Iraq leader Adel Mashadani arrested in Baghdad," *Los Angeles Times*, 29 March 2009; Ned Parker and Caesar Ahmed, "Sons of Iraq Movement Suffers another Blow," *Los Angeles Times*, 30 March 2009.

9.   Special Inspector General for Iraq Reconstruction, "Quarterly Report and Semiannual Report to the United States Congress" (30 January 2011), 70.

10. In January 2010, MNF-I reported that the Government of Iraq had integrated 41,000 Sons of Iraq, out of the 76,000 local forces on the payroll. In October 2009, the government had integrated only 16,300 Sons of Iraq into government. Less than 9,500 Sons of Iraq were integrated into the security forces. Major General Stephen Lanza interview with Al-Sumaria TV (11 January 2010); Special Inspector General for Iraq Reconstruction, "Quarterly Report to the United States Congress" (30 October 2009).

11. Gardiner, 157.

12. Akehurst, 63-64.

13. Najim Abed Al-Jabouri and Sterling Jensen, "The Iraqi and AQI roles in the Sunni Awakening," *Prism* 2, no. 1 (December 2010): 3-4.

14. The fact that Queens' Own Corps of Guides and the Firqat Salahdin were both initially mixed units that seem to provide exceptions to this conclusion. Leadership may be an important factor in explaining this phenomenon. Advisors for the Firqat Salahdin suggested that Salim Mubarak's leadership and charisma enabled the multi-tribal organization to overcome traditional rivalries. The Firqat Salahdin mutinied within 48 hours of Salim's death. Lumsden's leadership in the Guides seems to an influencing factor for building a unit that could transcend class issues in British India. The Firqat Salahdin mutinied within 48 hours of Salim's death. However, Lumsden lead the Guides for nearly 15 years.

15. The Govindgarh fortress had a regiment of Sikh infantry and at 18 guns protecting one of the approaches to Amritsar. The Guides devised a plan by which a small force would penetrate the fortress with part of their own posing as prisoners and their guards. The Guides gained entrance to the fortes, turned over their "prisoners", co-opted the garrison's commander, and loitered near the guardhouse. When the British forces neared, the Guides overpowered the guards and opened the fortress's gates for another force of Guides outside. The fortress was taken without any losses for the Guides. Younghusband, *The Story of the Guides*, 31-38.

16. David Chapman, *Security Forces of the Kurdistan Regional Government* (Costa Mesa: Mazda, 2011), 162-164.

17. Interview CF20110914DV0001_SESSION1A, 14 September 2011; Interview CF20110917DV0002_SESSION1A, 17 September 2011.

18. The term "green-on-blue" attack refers to attacks that involve coalition troops and host nation security forces. It is a form friendly-fire incident. Tim Lister, "Attacks by Afghan troops on NATO Soldiers rising, but motives complex," *CNN World*, 15 June 2011, http://www.cnn.com/2011/WORLD/asiapcf/06/14/afghanistan.nato.attacks/ index.html (accessed 10 November 2011).

19. The Pakistani Army's partnership with the Frontier Corps in the Federally Administered Tribal Areas (FATA) could be another important case study to understanding importance of this aspect of advisor duty. Following partition, Pakistan focused its military resources on the border shared with India, primarily the Line of Control in Kashmir. The Pakistani Army continues to second officers to the Frontier Corps, but most officers consider the duty a dead-end assignment. A 2008 study by the National Bureau of Asian Research and the Islamabad Policy Research Institute recommended that Pakistan officers sent to the Frontier Corps receive specialized training in mountain and counterinsurgency operations. Hassan Abbas, "Transforming Pakistan's Frontier Corps," *Terrorism Monitor* 5, no. 6 (March 2007): 5-8; Pervaiz Iqbal Cheema, "Challenges Facing a Counter-Militant Campaign in Pakistan's FATA," *NBR Analysis* 19, no. 3 (August 2008): 26-27.

20. Robert Gates, "A Balanced Strategy: Reprogramming the Pentagon for a New Age," *Foreign Affairs* 88, no. 1 (January/February 2009): 37.

21. A number of British officers have suggested that this oversight in Iraq is partially related to two important events. First, the military's emphasis remained focused on the British Army on the Rhine During the Cold War. Second, the Northern Ireland counterinsurgency created a number of institutional obstacles for sharing information, emerging doctrine, and best practices across units. Interviews with present and former British officers, 16 September 2011 and 21 September 2011. Additionally see Daniel P. Marston, "Adaption in the Field: The British Army's difficult Campaign in Iraq," *Security Challenges* 6, no. 1 (Autumn, 2010): 71-84 and Brigadier Richard Iron's upcoming article on the continuing influence of Northern Ireland on the British Army.

22. Countries with a liberal democratic tradition provided the trainers in the case studies presented. Further research should examine countries with more authoritarian governments to understand if this limitation is significant. Interview CB20110901G0001_SESSION1A, 1 September 2011.

Glossary

Adoo. An Arabic term for the enemy used during the Dhofar insurgency.

Arbakai. A tribal security force formed for the purpose of enforcing a jirga's decisions. The *arbakai* is unique to the Pushtun tribes in the Paktia province.

Badel. A Pushtunwali principle stating that a tribesman must exact vengeance for a wrong done to his family. The term is also referred to as a blood feud.

Firqat. An Arabic word loosely translates to "task force" or "company" in military terms; however, other translations suggest it may only mean "group" used during the Dhofar campaign.

Firqatman. A tribesman fighting with the *firqat* in Dhofar.

Foreign Internal Defense. In US joint doctrine, the participation by civilian and military agencies of a government in any of the action programs taken by another government or other designated organization, to free and protect its society from subversion, lawlessness, insurgency, terrorism, and other threats to their security.

Hamsayas. A Pushtun word for people who assist the tribesmen with the daily functioning of the tribes that are not necessarily Pushtun.

Harasis. A term used to describe the glottal dialect used by the tribes in Dhofar.

Imperial Policing. In UK doctrine, campaigns where civil control of the population does not exist, or has broken down to the extent where the military is the only institution that can provide security.

In Aid of the Civil Power. In UK doctrine, a campaign where the civil government maintains control but lacks the personnel numbers to provide adequate security for the populace. The military's duty is to provide assistance for the restoration of law and order during the disturbance.

Irregular Force. Armed individuals or groups who are not members of the regular armed forces, police, or other internal security forces.

Jebel. Arabic for mountain or hill.

Jebebi. A term used to describe the glottal dialect used by the tribes in **Dhofar**. The term also describes a person that lives on the jebel.

Jirga. Primary decision making body for both intra- and inter-tribal disputes in the Pushtun society.

Khareef. Arabic term for the southeast monsoon in Dhofar.

Lashkar. An irregular force or war party raised by a tribe or tribes to punish the party that violates the decision of a *jirga*, or commits a violation contrary to the *Pukhtonwali* code.

Melmastia. A Pushtunwali principle stating a requirement for hospitality.

Military Capability Building. In UK doctrine, the range of activities in support of developing an indigenous security force including partnering, monitoring, mentoring, and training.

Nanawati. A Pushtunwali principle stating that any man can request asylum in the presence of the Koran and that request cannot be denied.

Negd. The desert region north of the jebel in Dhofar. Refers to the region known as the Empty Quarter Desert.

Operation EMU. The operational name given to the mission of raising the *firqat* in Dhofar by the British Army and the Sultan's Armed Forces.

Operation STORM. The operational name given to the mission of defeating the insurgency in Dhofar by the British Army and the Sultan's Armed Forces. It was comprised of five fronts.

Operation TELIC. The operational name under which all British military operations in Iraq were conducted between the invasion of Iraq on 19 March 2003 and the withdrawal of the last remaining British forces on 22 May 2011.

Pagri. Hindu term for a long piece of cloth that must be manually tied into a headdress. The color of the headdress can indicate the wearer's caste.

Population Control. In US Army doctrine, determining who lives in an area and what they do.

Pushtunwali. An unwritten system of principles that govern individual and collective relations between members of the Pushtun and Pukhtun tribes.

Security Force Assistance. In US joint doctrine, the unified action to generate, employ, and sustain local, Host Nation, or regional security forces in support of a legitimate authority.

Security Sector Reform. In UK doctrine, a specific program of activities coordinated to create capable indigenous security forces (police and armed forces) generally tailored to a specific theatre.

Small War. In UK doctrine, all campaigns other than those where both the opposing sides consist of regular troops. In US Marine Corps doctrine, an operation undertaken under executive authority, wherein military force is combined with diplomatic pressure in the internal or external affairs of another state whose government is unstable, inadequate, or unsatisfactory for the preservation of life and of such interests as are determined by the foreign policy of our Nation.

Wali. Governor of a province or region in Oman.

Watch and Ward. The informal term used by the Indian Army for the mission of guarding the frontier.

Bibliography

Primary Sources

Oriental and India Office Collections

Browne Mss Papers of General Sir Samuel James Browne, MSS Eur F486.

Cummings Mss Papers of Maj. Walter James Cummings, MSS Eur Photo Eur 437.

India Military Proceedings (India Office Records and Private Papers), IOR/P/1-12828.

Keyes Mss Papers of General Sir Charles Patton Keyes, MSS Eur D1084.

Military Department Library, IOR/L.MIL/17.

Montagu Mss Papers of Edwin Samuel Montagu, Mss Eur D523/9.

Political and Secret Memoranda, IOR/L/PandS/18.

Liddell Hart Centre for Military Archives

Campbell Mss Papers of General Sir Frederick Campbell Collection.

Deane-Drummond Mss Papers of Major General Anthony John Deane-Drummond Collection.

Thwaites Mss Papers of Brig Peter Trevenan Thwaites Collection.

Middle East Centre, St. Antony's College Oxford

John David Carew Graham Collection, GB165-0327.

J. H. McKeown Collection, GB165-0339.

Pauline Searle Collection, GB165-0328.

Veteran Interviews–United Kingdom

CF20110912J0001_SESSION1A. Former SAS Squadron Commander. Interview by Majors Michael Gunther, Eric Haas, Michael Stewart, Marcus Welch, and Darrell Vaughan, Warminster, 12 September 2011.

CF20110913C0001_SESSION1A. Former SAS Squadron Commander. Interview by Majors Michael Gunther, Eric Haas, Michael Stewart, Marcus Welch, and Darrell Vaughan, Warminster, 13 September 2011.

CF20110914DV0001_SESSION1A. Group interview with five Dhofar veterans including two former SAF regimental commanders, one BATT veteran, one BATT, Firqat Force, and civil aid veteran, and one psyops Soldier. Interview by Majors Michael Gunther, Eric Haas, Michael Stewart, Marcus Welch, and Darrell Vaughan, Warminster, 14 September 2011.

CF20110914DV0001_SESSION2A. Group interview with two former SAF regimental commanders. Interview by Major Eric Haas, Warminster, 14 September 2011.

CF20110914MS0001_SESSION1A. Group interview with two Dhofar veterans including one BATT veteran, and one BATT, Firqat Force, and civil aid veteran. Interview by author, Warminster, 14 September 2011.

CF20110917DV0002_SESSION1A. Group interview with two Dhofar veterans including one BATT and Firqat Force officer and one contract SAF officer. Interview by Majors Michael Gunther, Eric Haas, Michael Stewart, Marcus Welch, and Darrell Vaughan, Oxford, 17 September 2011.

CF20110917DV0002_SESSION2A. Continuation of group interview CF20110917DV0002_SESSION1A, Oxford, 17 September 2011.

CF2011091810001_SESSION1A. Interview of former UK general officer. Interview by Majors Michael Gunther, Eric Haas, Michael Stewart, Marcus Welch, and Darrell Vaughan, Oxford, 18 September 2011.

Veteran Interviews – United States

CB20110901G0001_SESSION1A. Interview with former Division chief of staff and US Brigade Commander, interview by Major Eric Haas, Fort Leavenworth, KS., 1 September 2011.

CB20110830M0001_SESSION1A. Interview with former US Brigade Commander, interview by author, Fort Leavenworth, KS., 30 August 2011.

Official Publications

Baker, III, James A., and Lee H. Hamilton, eds. *The Iraq Study Group Report: The Way Forward – A New Approach.* New York: Vintage, 2006.

"The Exchange of Letters between the Government of the United Kingdom of Great Britain and Northern Ireland and the Sultan of Muscat and Oman concerning the Sultan's Armed Forces, Civil Aviation, Royal Air Force facilities and Economic Development in Muscat and Oman, London 25 July 1958" HMSO Cmnd. 507, Treaty Series No. 28. London: HMSO, 1958.

Military Support of Law Enforcement during Civil Disturbances: A Report Concerning the California National Guard's Part in Suppressing the Los Angeles Riot, August 1965. Sacramento: California Office of State Printing, 1966.

Report of the Commissioners Appointed to Inquire into the Organization of the Indian Army; together with Minutes and Appendix. London: HMSO, 1859.

Special Inspector General for Iraq Reconstruction. "Quarterly Report to the United States Congress" 30 October 2009.

―――. "Quarterly Report and Semiannual Report to the United States Congress" 30 January 2011.

Taizi, Sherzaman. *Jirga System in Tribal Life*. Williamsburg: Tribal Analysis Center, 2007.

Temple, Richard. *Report Showing the Relations of the British Government with the Tribes, Independent and Dependent, on the North-West Frontier of the Punjab from the Annexation in 1849 to the close of 1855*. Calcutta: District Memorandum, 1855.

Military Publications

Standing Orders of the Punjab Frontier Force: Corrected to January 1, 1889. 2 vols. Silma: Government Central Press, 1889.

Department of the Army. Field Manual 1-02 *Operational Terms and Graphics*. Washington, DC: Government Printing Office, 21 September 2004.

―――. Field Manual 3-0 *Operations* (Change 1). Washington, DC: Headquarters, Department of the Army, 22 February 2011.

―――. Field Manual 3-07 *Stability Operations*. Ann Arbor: University of Michigan Press, 2009.

―――. Field Manual 3-07.1 *Security Force Assistance*. Washington, DC: Government Printing Office, 1 May 2009.

―――. Field Manual 3-24 *Counterinsurgency*. Chicago: University of Chicago Press, 2007.

―――. Field Manual 3-24.2 *Tactics in Counterinsurgency*. Washington, DC: Government Printing Office, 21 April 2009.

―――. Field Manual 7-98 *Operations in Low Intensity Conflict*. Washington, DC: Government Printing Office, 19 October 1992.

―――. Field Manual 90-8 *Counterguerrilla Operations*. Washington, DC: Government Printing Office, 29 August 1986.

―――. Field Manual Interim 3-07.22 *Counterinsurgency Operations*. Washington, DC: Government Printing Office, 1 October 2006.

Department of Defense. Joint Publication 3-22 *Foreign Internal Defense*. Washington, DC: Government Printing Office, 12 July 2010.

Headquarters, International Security Assistance Force. "ISAF

Commander's Counterinsurgency Guidance" Kabul, 25 August 2009.

Ministry of Defence. British Army Field Manual Volume 1 Part 10 *Countering Insurgency*. London: Ministry of Defence, October 2009.

————. Land Operations Volume III–*Counter Revolutionary Operations, Part 1–General Principles*. Manchester: HM Stationary Office Press, 1977.

United States Marine Corps. *Small Wars Manual, 1940*. Washington, DC: Government Printing Office, 1940.

War Office, *Imperial Policing and Duties in Aid of the Civil Power, 1949*. London: Fosh and Cross Ltd., 1949.

————. *Keeping the Peace, Part 1–Doctrine*. Manchester: HM Stationary Office Press, 1963.

Memoirs

Akehurst, John. *We Won a War*. Guildford: Briddles Limited, 1982.

Allfree, P. S. *Warlords of Oman*. London: Robert Hale, 2008.

Arkless, David C. *The Secret War*. London: William Limbar, 1988.

Burruss, Lewis. *Mike Force*. Lincoln: Pocketbooks, 1989.

Churchill, Winston. *The Story of the Malakand Field Force: An Episode of Frontier War*. London: Thomas Nelson and Sons, 1916.

Cumming, Walter James. *Frontier Fighters: On Active Service in Waziristan*. Edited by Jules Stewart. Barnsley: Pen and Sword Military, 2010.

Fiennes, Ranulph. *Living Dangerously*. London: Athenaeum, 1988.

Forrest, G. W. *The Life of Field Marshall Sir Neville Chamberlain*. London: William Blackwood and Sons, 1909.

Galula, David. *Counterinsurgency Warfare: Theory and Practice*. Westport: Praeger Security International, 1964.

Gardiner, Ian. *In the Service of the Sultan*. Yorkshire: Pen and Sword Books, 2007.

Gough, Charles and Arthur Innes. *The Sikhs and the Sikh Wars*. London: A.D. Innes and Co., 1897.

Jeapes, Tony. *SAS Secret War: Operation Storm in the Middle East*. Mechanicsburg: Stackpole Books, 1996.

Kitson, Frank. *Bunch of Five*. London: Faber and Faber, 1977.

Lawrence-Archer, James Henry. *Commentaries of the Punjab Campaign 1848-49* London: Wm.H. Allen andand Co., 1878.

Lumsden, Peter S., and George R. Elsmie. *Lumsden of the Guides: A Sketch of the Life of Lieut.-Gen. Sir Harry Burnett Lumsden, K.C.S.I., C.B., with Selections from his Correspondence and Occasional Papers.* London: John Murray, 1900.

MacGregor, Lady, ed. *The Life and Opinions of Maj Gen Sir Charles Metcalfe MacGregor*, 2 vols. London: W. Blackwood and Sons, 1888.

Nevill, H. L. *Campaigns on the North-West Frontier*. London: John Murray, 1912.

Peterson, Michael E. *The Combined Action Platoons: The US Marines' Other War in Vietnam*. New York: Praeger, 1989.

Purdon, Corran. *List the Bugle: Reminiscences of an Irish Soldier*. Antrim: Greystone Books, Ltd., 1993.

Ray, Bryan. *Dangerous Fontiers: Campaigning in Somaliland and Oman.* Barnsley: Pen and Sword Military, 2008.

Roberts, Frederick. *Forty-One Years in India: From Subaltern to Commander in Chief*, 2 vols. London: Richard Bentley and Sons, 1897.

Sibley, Paul. *A Monk in the SAS*. London: Spiderwize, 2011.

Skeen, Andrew. *Passing It On: Fighting the Pushtun of Afghanistan's Frontier*. Fort Leavenworth: Foreign Military Studies Office, 2010.

Smiley, David. *Arabian Assignment*. London: Cooper, 1975.

Thompson, Robert. *Defeating Communist Insurgency*. St. Petersburg: Hailer Publishing, 1966.

Trinquier, Roger. *Modern Warfare: A French View of Counterinsurgency.* Westport: Praeger Security International, 1964.

Vaughan, J. Luther. *My Service in the Indian Army–and After*. London: Archibald Constable and Co. Ltd., 1904.

Villiers-Stuart, J. P. *Letters of a Once Punjab Frontier Force Officer.* London: Sifton Praed and Co., Ltd., 1925.

Younghusband, George John. *Indian Frontier Warfare*. London: Kegan Paul, Trench, Trübner and Co., 1898.

———. *The Story of the Guides*. London: MacMillan and Co., 1908.

Regimental Histories

History of the 5th Royal Gurkha Rifles (Frontier Force). Aldershot: Gale and Polden, 1929.

History of the Guides, 1846-1922. Aldershot: Gale and Polden, 1938.

Condon, W. E. H. *The Frontier Force Regiment*. Aldershot: Gale and Polden, 1962.

———. *The Frontier Force Rifles*. Aldershot: Gale and Polden, 1953.

Dey, Rai Sahib Boydo Nath. *A Brief Account of the Punjab Frontier Force: From its organization in 1849 to its re-distribution on 31st March 1903*. Calcutta: W. Newman and Co., 1905.

Gorman, J. T. *2nd Battalion, 4th Bombay Grenadiers, King Edward's Own, formerly the 102nd King Edward's Own Grenadiers. Historical record of the regiment, 1796-1933*. Weston-super-Mare: Lawrence Bros., 1933.

Lindsay, D. M. *Regimental History of the 6th Royal Battalion (Scinde) 13th Frontier Force Rifles, 1843-1934*. Aldershot: Gale and Polden, Ltd., 1935.

Wylly, H. C. *History of the 5th Battalion 13th Frontier Force Rifles*. Eastborne: Antony Rowe Ltd, 1929.

Secondary Sources

Books

Allen, Jr., Calvin, and W. Lynn Rigsbee, II, *Oman Under Qaboos: From Coup to Constitution, 1970-1996*. London: Frank Cass, 2000.

Ambrose, Stephen. *Nixon: The Triumph of a Politician 1962-1972*, Vol. 2. New York: Simon and Schuster, 1989.

Baha, Lal. *NWFP Administration under British Rule 1901-1919*. Islamabad: National Commission on Historical and Cultural Research, 1978.

Bayly, Susan. "Caste and Race in the Colonial Ethnography of India," In *The Concept of Race in South Asia*, edited by Peter Robb, 165-218. London: School of Oriental and African Studies, 1998.

Berman, Paul. *Terror and Liberalism*. New York: W.W. Norton and Company, 2004.

Bruner, Edward F. *Military Forces: What is the Appropriate Size for the United States?* Washington, DC: Congressional Research Service, 10 February 2005.

Callwell, C. E. *Small Wars: Their Principles and Practice*, 3rd ed. London: HM Stationary Press, 1906.

Calvocoressi, Peter. *World Politics Since 1945*. 9th ed. Harlow: Pearson Education Limited, 2009.

Caroe, Olaf. *The Pathans*. 1958. Reprint. Karachi: Oxford University Press, 1988.

Carver, Michael. *The Seven Ages of the British Army*. New York: Beaufort Books. Inc, 1984.

Center for Technology and National Security Policy. *Transforming for Stabilization and Reconstruction Operations*. Washington, DC: National Defense University, 12 November 2003.

Chapman, David. *Security Forces of the Kurdistan Regional Government*. Costa Mesa: Mazda, 2011.

Clausewitz, Carl von. *On War*. Edited and translated by Michael Howard and Peter Paret. Princeton: Princeton University Press, 1976.

Cole, Roger, and Richard Belfield. *SAS Operation Storm: Nine Men Against Four Hundred in Britain's Secret War*. London: Hodder and Stoughton Ltd., 2011.

Corum, James. *Training Indigenous Forces in Counterinsurgency: A Tale of Two Insurgencies*. Carlisle: Strategic Studies Institute, March 2006.

Dalrymple, William. *The Last Mughal: The Fall of Delhi, 1957*. New York: Bloomsbury, 2006.

Farwell, Byron. *The Great Boer War*. New York: Harper and Row, 1976.

Gould, Lewis L. *1968: The Election that Changed America*. Chicago: Ivan R. Dee, 1993.

Gwynn, Charles W. *Imperial Policing*. London: MacMillan and Co., Ltd., 1936.

Heathcote, T. A. *The Indian Army*. London: David and Charles, 1974.

Holmes, Richard. *Sahibs: The British Soldier in India*. London: Haprer Press, 2006.

Hopkirk, Peter. *The Great Game: The Struggle for Empire in Central Asia*. London: John Murray, 1990.

Horne, Gerald. *Fire This Time: The Watts Uprising and the 1960s*. Charlottesville: University Press of Virginia, 1995.

Innes, James John McLeod. *Sir Henry Lawrence: The Pacificator*. Oxford: Clarendon Press, 1898.

James, Lawrence. *Raj: The Making and Unmaking of British India*. New York: St. Martin's Press, 1997.

Janzen, Jorg. "The Destruction of Resources among the Mountain Nomads of Dhofar." In *The Transformation of Nomadic Society in the Arab East,* edited by Martha Mundy and Basim Musallam, 130-171. Cambridge: Cambridge University Press, 2000.

Kagan, Kimberly. *The Surge: A Military History*. New York: Encounter Books, 2009.

Kilcullen, David. *The Accidental Guerrilla: Fighting Small Wars in the Midst of a Big One*. Oxford: Oxford University Press, 2009.

———. *Counterinsurgency*. Oxford: Oxford University Press, 2010.

Kneece Jr., R. Royce. *Force Sizing for Stability Operations*. Alexandria: Institute for Defense Analyses, 2010.

Linn, Brian. *The Philippine War, 1899-1902*. Lawrence: University of Kansas Press, 2000.

Locke, John. *The Works of John Locke*, 10 vols. London: W. Sharpe and Son, 1823.

Luttwak, Edward. *Grand Strategy of the Roman Empire*. Baltimore: John Hopkins University Press, 1979.

Mackinlay, John. *Insurgent Archipelago*. New York: Columbia University Press, 2009.

MacMunn, George. *The Armies of India*. London: Adam and Charles Black, 1911.

———. *Martial Races of India*. London: Low and Marston, 1933.

———. *The Romance of the Indian Frontiers*. London: Jonathan Cape, Ltd., 1931.

———. *Vignettes from Indian Wars*. London: Sampson Low, Marston and Co., 1901.

Mao Tse-Tung, *Guerrilla Warfare*. Translated by Samuel B. Griffith II. Chicago: University of Illinois Press, 2000.

Marston, Daniel P. *Phoenix from the Ashes: The Indian Army in the Burma Campaign*. Westport CT: Preager, 2003.

Marston, Daniel P., and Carter Malkasian, eds. *Counterinsurgency in the Modern Warfare*. Long Island City: Osprey, 2010.

Marston, Daniel P., and Chandar Sundraham, eds. *A Military History of India and South Asia*. Westport Ct: Preager, 2007.

Mason, Philip. *A Matter of Honor: An Account of the Indian Army, Its Officers and Men*. London: Papermac, 1986.

Mataxis, Thomas C. "The Afghan Insurgency and the Reagan Doctrine." In *The History of Guerrilla Warfare*. Ann Arbor: XanEdu, 1994.

Mazumder, Rajit. *The Indian Army and the Making of the Punjab*. New Dehli: Sapra Brothers, 2011.

McCoy, Alfred. *Policing America's Empire*. Madison: University of Wisconsin Press, 2009.

Mill, John Stuart. *On Liberty*. 1859. Reprint. New York: Dover Publications, 2002.

Moreman, T. R. *The Army in India and the Development of Frontier Warfare*. Houndmills: Palgrave, 1998.

Morgenthau, Hans J. *Politics Among Nations: The Struggle for Power and Peace* 7th ed. New York: McGraw-Hill, 2006.

Omissi, David. *The Sepoy and the Raj: The Indian Army 1860-1940*. Basingstoke: Routledge Publishers, 1994.

Peterson, J. E. *Oman's Insurgencies: The Sultanate's Struggle for Supremacy*. London: SAQI, 2007.

Price, D. L. "Oman: Insurgency and Development". London: Institute for the Study of Conflict, 1975.

Rabasa, Angel, Lesley Anne Warner, Peter Chalk, Ivan Khilko, and Paraag Skula. *Money in the Bank: Lessons Learned from Past Counterinsurgency (COIN) Operations*. Arlington: RAND Corporation, 2007.

Raverty, H. G. *A Dictionary of the Pukhto-Pushto or Language of the Afghans*. Ottawa: Laurier Books Ltd., 2001.

Ricks, Thomas E. *The Gamble: General Petraeus and the American Military Adventure in Iraq*. New York: Penguin Books, 2009.

Rose, Sumantra. *Kashmir: Roots of Conflict, Paths to Peace*. Cambridge: Harvard University Press: 2005.

Rosen, Stephen Peter. *Societies and Military Power: India and its Armies*. Ithaca: Cornell University Press, 1996.

Smith, Reginald Bosworth. *Life of Lord Lawrence,* 2 vols. London: Smith Elder and Co., 1883.

Smith, Rupert .*The Utility of Force: The Art of War in the Modern World.* New York: Vintage Books, 2007.

Streets, Heather. *Martial Races: The Military, Race, and Masculinity in the British Imperial Culture, 1857-1914.* Manchester: Manchester University Press, 2004.

Swinson, Arthur. *North-West Frontier.* London: Hutchinson and Co., Ltd., 1967.

Tan Tai Yong. *The Garrison State: The Military, Government and Society in Colonial Punjab, 1949-1947.* London: SAGE Publications, 2005.

Tierney Jr., John. *Chasing Ghosts: Unconventional Warfare in American History.* Dulles: Potomac Books, 2006.

Townsend, John. *Oman: Making of a Modern State.* London: C. Helm, 1977.

Trench, Charles Chenevix. *The Frontier Scouts.* London: Jonathan Cape Ltd, 1985.

Tripodi, Christian. *Edge of Empire: The British Political Officer and Tribal Administration on the North-West Frontier, 1877-1947.* Farnham: Ashgate, 2011.

Upton, Emory. *The Armies of Asia and Europe.* New York: D Appleton and Co., 1878.

Utley, Robert M. *Frontier Regulars: The United States Army and the Indian, 1866-1891.* Lincoln: University of Nebraska Press, 1973.

Vegetius, Flavius. *De Re Militari.* Translated by John Clarke. London: 1767.

Woodruff, Philip. *The Men Who Ruled India: Volume II, The Guardians.* London: Jonathan Cape, 1963.

Yergin, Daniel. *The Prize: The Epic Quest for Oil, Money, and Power.* New York: Simon and Shuster, 2008.

Journals

Abbas, Hassan. "Transforming Pakistan's Frontier Corps." *Terrorism Monitor* 5, no. 6 (March 2007): 5-8.

Carter, Nick, and Alexander Alderson. "Partnering with Local Forces." *The RUSI Journal* 156, no. 3 (2011): 34-40.

Cheema, Pervaiz Iqbal. "Challenges Facing a Counter-Militant Campaign in Pakistan's FATA." *NBR Analysis* 19, no. 3 (August 2008): 21-29.

Cohen, Stephen. "The Untouchable Soldier: Caste, Politics, and the Indian Army." *Journal of Asian Studies* 28, no. 3 (May 1969): 453-468.

Ganguly, Sumit. "Explaining the Kashmir Insurgency: Political Mobilization and Institutional Decay." *International Security* 21, no. 2 (Autumn 1996): 76-107.

Gates, Robert M. "A Balanced Strategy: Reprogramming the Pentagon for a New Age." *Foreign Affairs* 88, no. 1 (January/February 2009): 28-40.

———. "Helping Others Defend Themselves: The Future of US Security Assistance." *Foreign Affairs* (May/June 2010): 2-6.

Greenhut, Jeffrey. "Sahib and Sepoy: An Inquiry into the Relationship between the British Officers and Native Soldiers of the British Indian Army." *Military Affairs* 48, no. 1 (January 1984): 15-18.

Hack, Karl. "The Malayan Emergency as Counter-Insurgency Paradigm." *Journal of Strategic Studies*, 32, no. 3 (June 2009): 383-414.

Johnson, Thomas, and M.Chris Mason. "No Sign until the Burst of Fire: Understanding the Pakistan-Afghanistan Frontier." *International Security* 32, no. 4 (Spring 2008): 41-77.

Krause, Peter J. P. "Troop Levels in Stability Operations: What We Don't Know." *Center for International Studies* (2007): 1-3.

Ladwig III, Walter C. "Supporting allies in counterinsurgency: Britain and the Dhofar Rebellion." *Small Wars and Insurgencies*, 19: no. 1 (2008): 62-88.

Lawrence, T. E. "Twenty-Seven Articles." *The Arab Bulletin*, 20 August 1917.

Marston, Daniel. "Adaptation in the Field: The British Army's Difficult Campaign in Iraq." *Security Challenges* 6, no. 1 (Autumn 2010): 78-81.

McKeown, John. "Britain and Oman: The Dhofar War and its Significance." M.Phil thesis, University of Cambridge, 1981.

Melamid, Alexander. "Dhofar." *Geographical Review* 74, no. 1 (January 1984): 106-109.

Najim Abed Al-Jabouri and Sterling Jensen, "The Iraqi and AQI roles in the Sunni Awakening." *Prism* 2, no. 1 (December 2010): 3-18.

Omrani, Bijan."The Durand Line: History and Problems of the Afghan-Pakistan Border." *Asian Affairs* 40, no. 2 (2009): 177-195.

Quinlivan, James. "Force Requirements in Stability Operations." *Parameters* 25 (Winter 1995-1996): 59-69.

Roy, Kausik. "The Construction of Regiments in the Indian Army: 1859-1913." *War in History* 8, no. 2 (2001): 127-148.

Skuy, David. "Macaulay and the Indian Penal Code of 1862: The Myth of the Inherent Superiority and Modernity of the English Legal System Compared to India's Legal System in the Nineteenth Century." *Modern Asian Studies* 32, no. 3 (1998): 513-557.

Tripodi, Christian. "'Good for one but not the other'; The Sandeman System of Pacification as Applied to Baluchistan and the North-West Frontier, 1877-1947." *The Journal of Military History* 73, no. 3 (July 2009): 767-802.

Varshney, Ashutosh. "India, Pakistan, and Kashmir: Antimonies of Nationalism." *Asian Survey* 31, no. 11 (November 1991): 997-1019.

News Articles

"A Nation Challenged: The President; Bush to Increase Federal Role in Security at Airports." *The New York Times*, 28 September 2001.

Lister, Tim. "Attacks by Afghan troops on NATO Soldiers rising, but motives complex." *CNN World*, 15 June 2011. http://www.cnn.com/2011/WORLD/asiapcf/06/14/ afghanistan.nato.attacks/index.html (accessed 10 November 2011).

Parker, Ned, and Usama Redha. "Sons of Iraq leader Adel Mashadani arrested in Baghdad." *Los Angeles Times*, 29 March 2009.

Parker, Ned, and Caesar Ahmed. "Sons of Iraq Movement Suffers another Blow." *Los Angeles Times*, 30 March 2009.

Rubin, Allissa J., and Richard A. Opeel, Jr. "US and Afghanistan Debate More Village Forces." *The New York Times*, 12 July 2010.

www.ingramcontent.com/pod-product-compliance
Lightning Source LLC
Chambersburg PA
CBHW081418090426

42738CB00017B/3407